THREADS
The Art of the Tear — Sparking the Imagination

Bespoke Bionics: The Artistry of Intelligence: VOLUME 02

"Bespoke Bionics" emerges as a visionary design concept, blending the timeless charm of traditional craftsmanship with the cutting-edge capabilities of modern technology. This concept envisions a realm where the aesthetics of handcrafted art and the functionality of technology harmonize, creating not just tools, but masterpieces of design.

Throughout history, human hands have shaped materials into artifacts of such complexity and beauty that they transcend their era, becoming timeless treasures. These objects, wrought from the earth and fired in kilns, painted by candlelight and polished by the dedicated hands of artisans, have always been the benchmarks of cultural ingenuity. They whisper tales of how civilizations strived for beauty in the everyday, how form was never sacrificed for function, and how each curve, contour, and color was a testament to the artisan's skill.

In this age, materials like silicon and steel are as significant as the clay and marble of old. "Bespoke Bionics" represents the next frontier where technology is not merely integrated into our daily lives but elevated to an art form. This design philosophy transcends ordinary mechanical constructs, offering instead a collection of artfully sculpted androids where every feature is meticulously designed for aesthetic elegance and functional brilliance.

In this innovative approach, robots are not assembled; they are crafted, born from a synthesis of antique artisanship and futuristic vision. Gears and circuits are interwoven with ornamental filigree and fine porcelain, creating beings that are as capable as they are enchanting. Every component, from joints to sensors to lines of code, is refined to achieve perfection, echoing the revered qualities of historic artifacts.

"Bespoke Bionics" celebrates the ingenious spirit of human creativity. This concept invites you to envision a gallery of the future where appreciation extends beyond functionality to the inherent beauty of design. It imagines robotics painted with a new brush of artistry, promising a future where machines not only think and act but do so with an elegance inspired by the human touch.

Welcome to the age of "Bespoke Bionics," where each creation is a masterpiece, every functionality is an expression, and every innovation is a continuation of our crafted past.

Copyright ©, Marigrace Hobbs MG Visual. All rights reserved. No part of this book may be reproduced or transmitted in any form or by any means, electronic or mechanical, including photocopying, recording, or by any information storage and retrieval system, without written permission from the publisher. ISBN: 978-1-964025-07-0

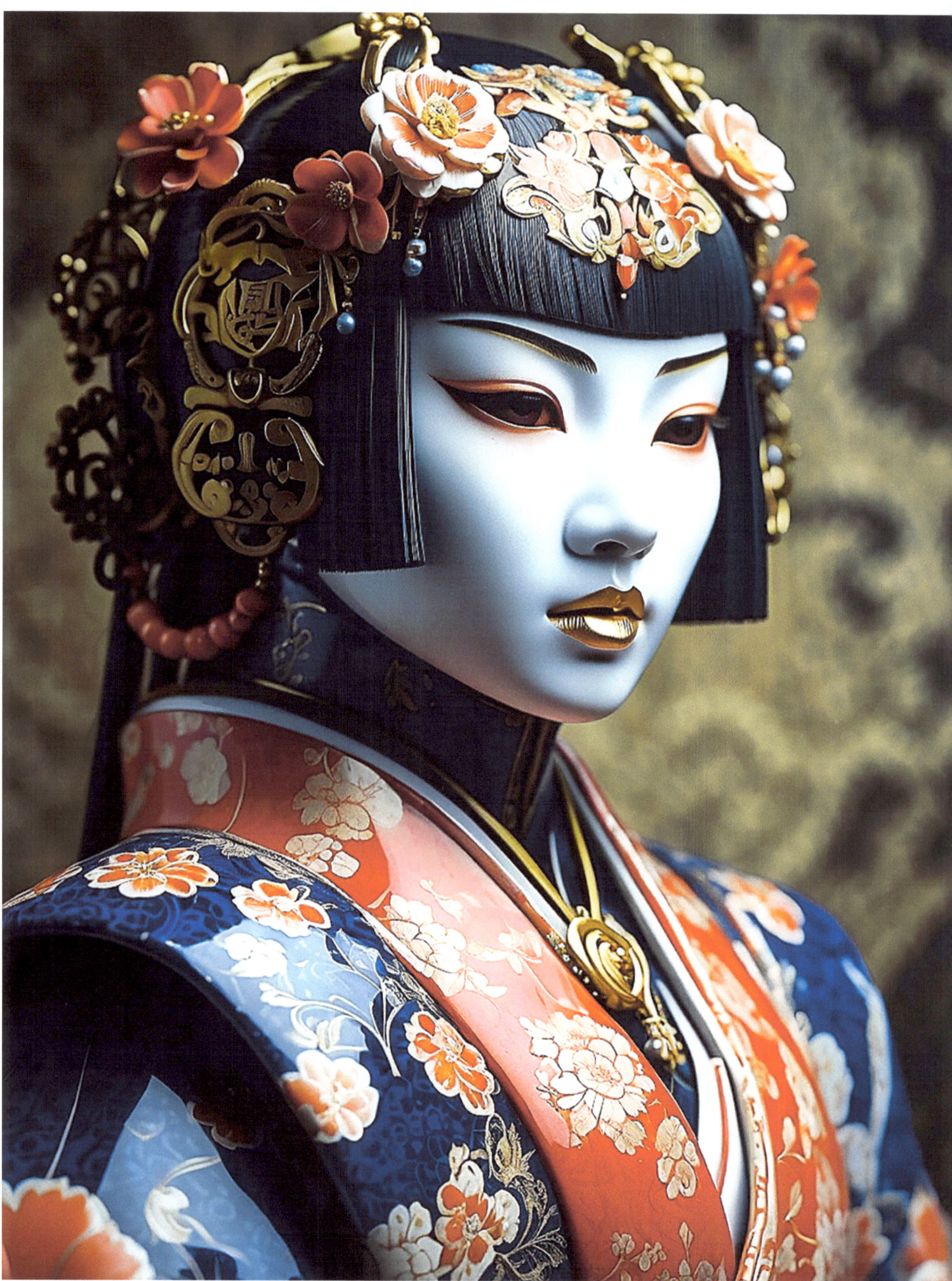

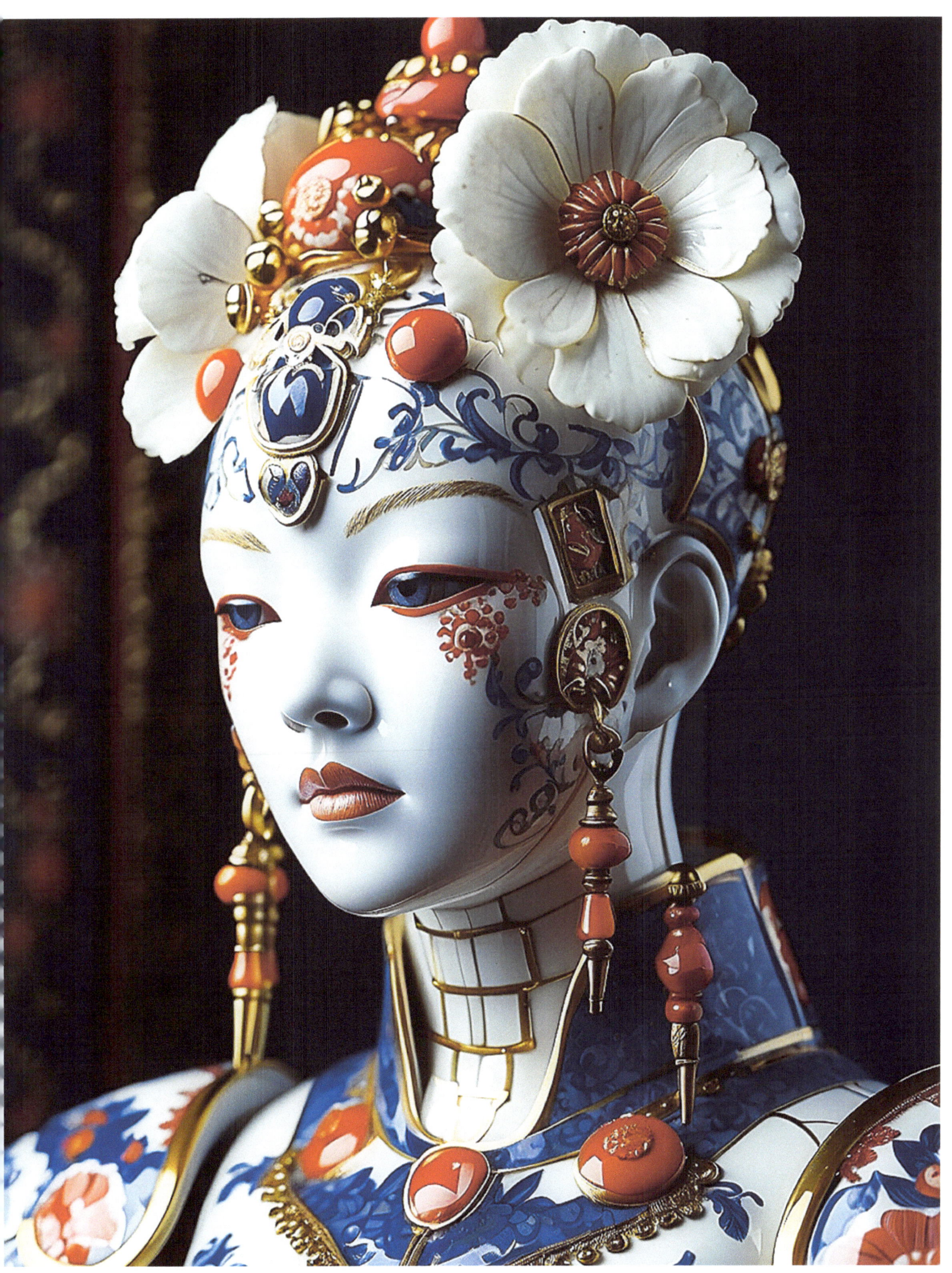

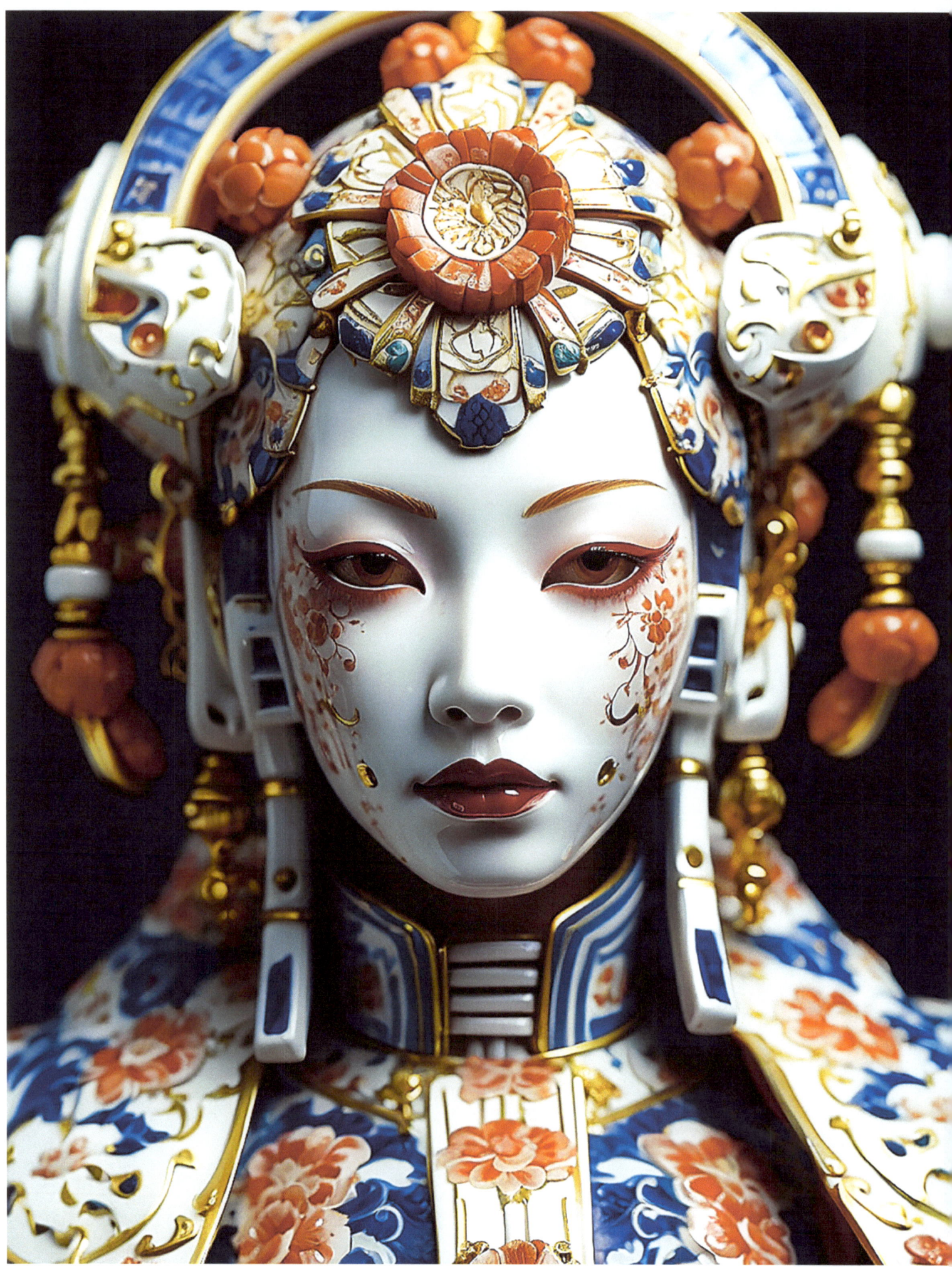

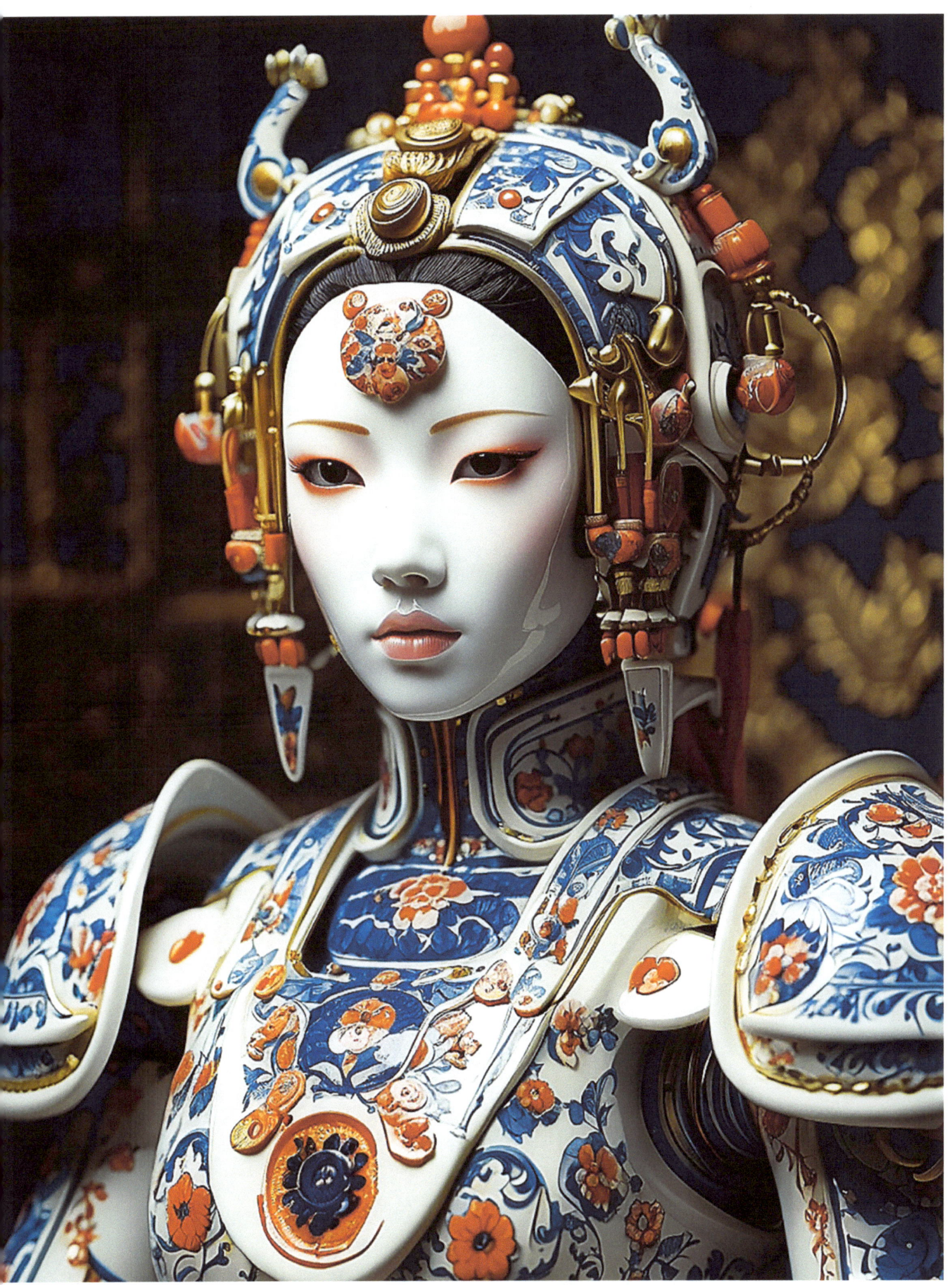

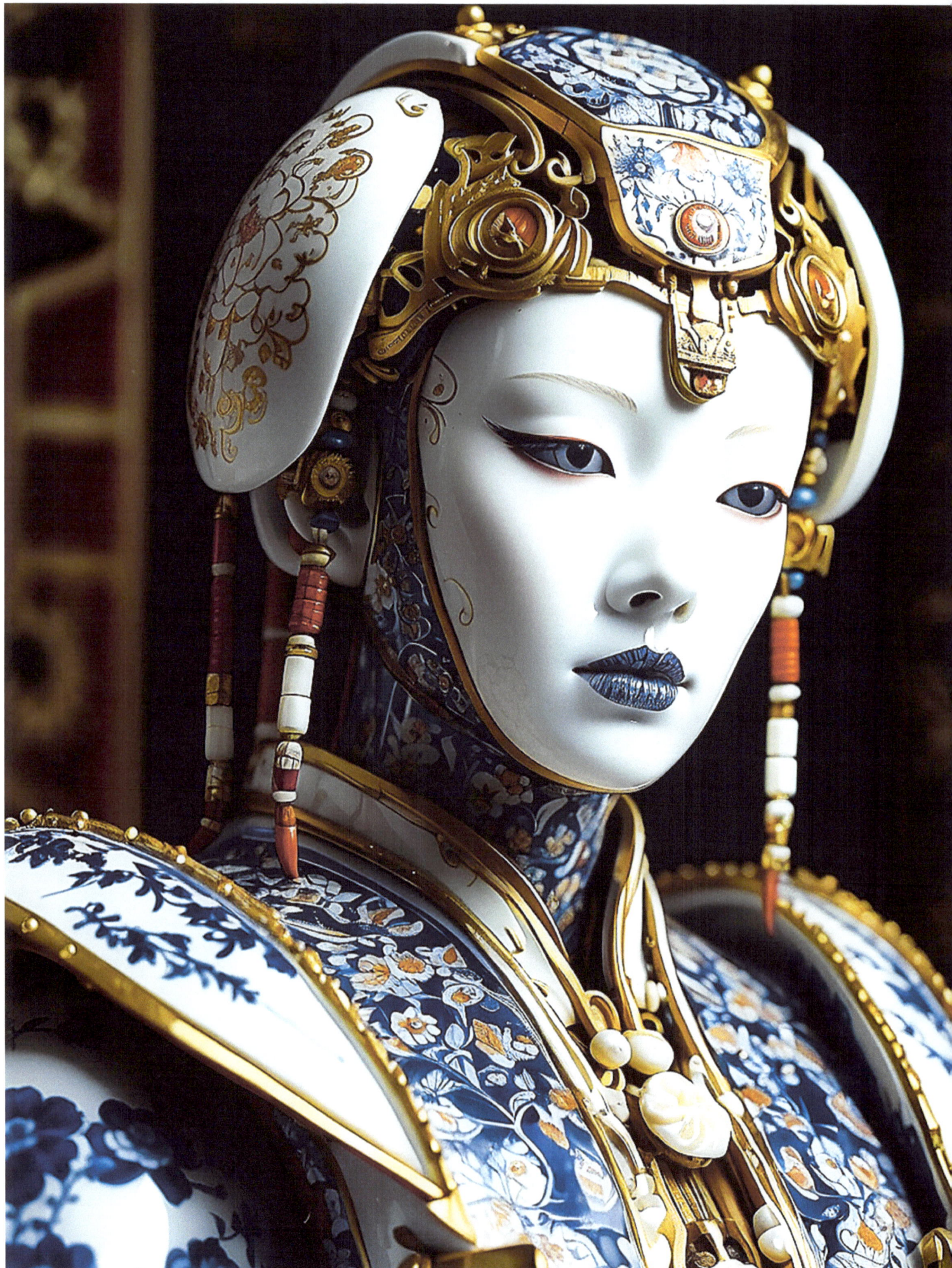

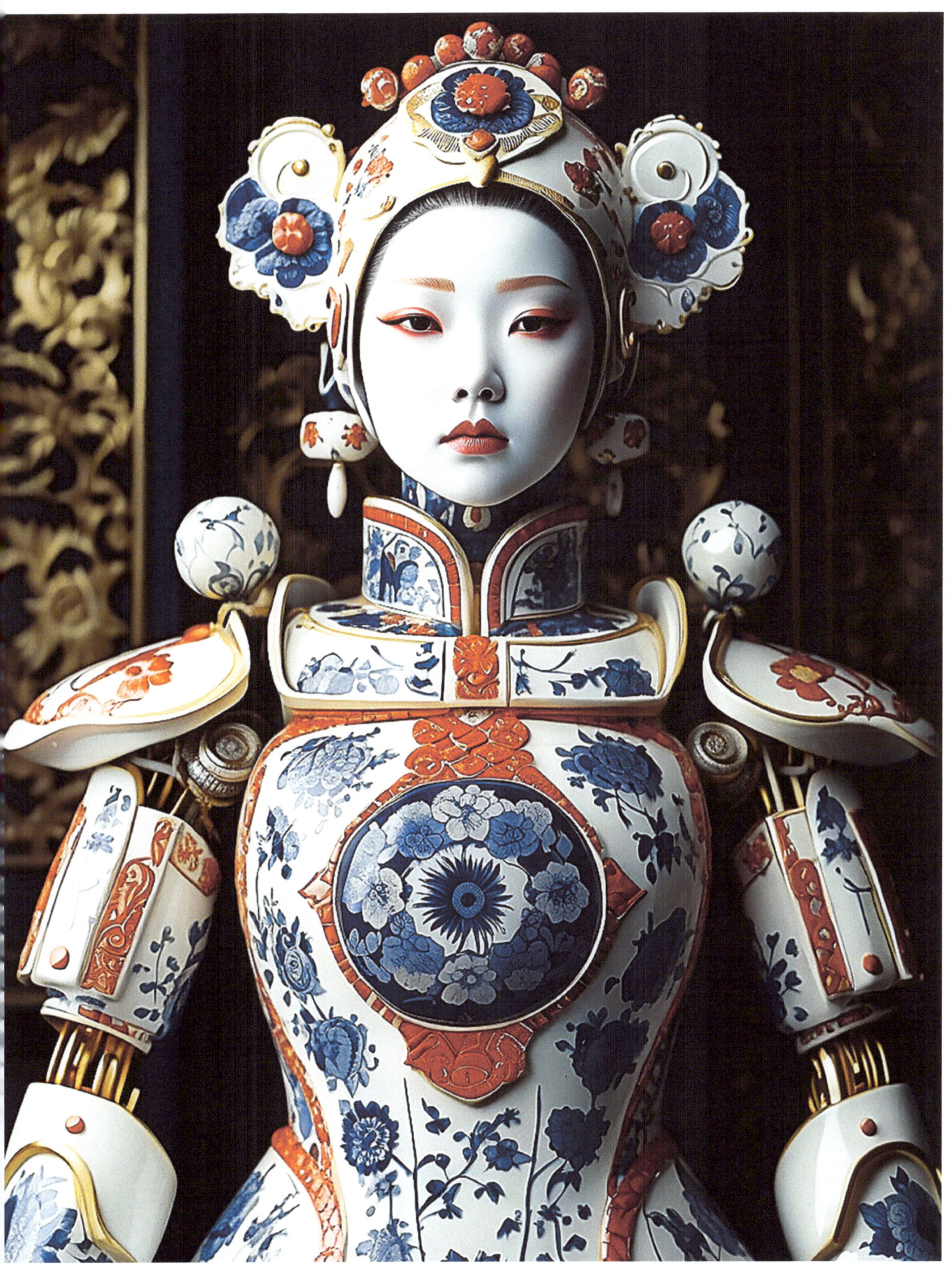

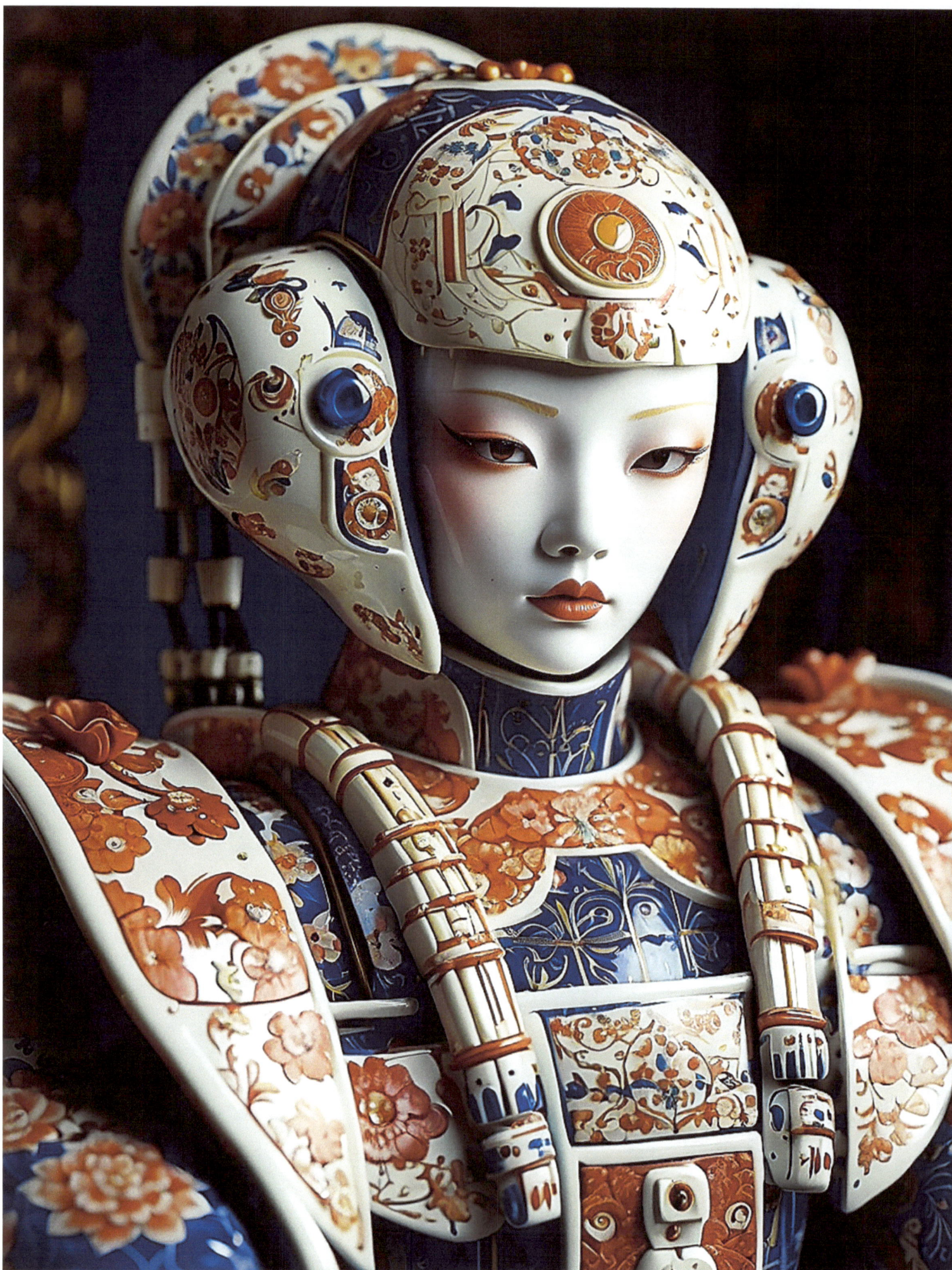

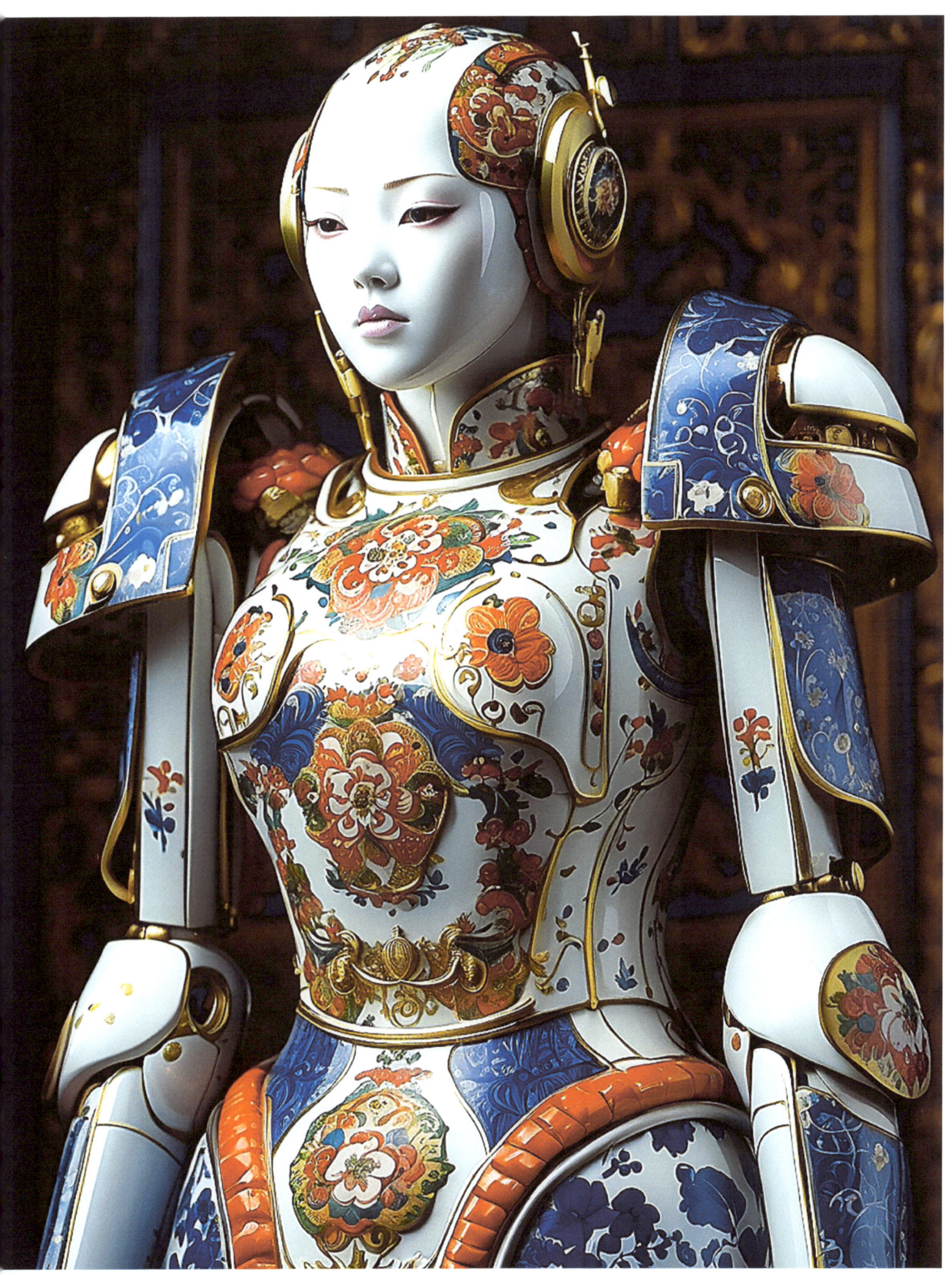

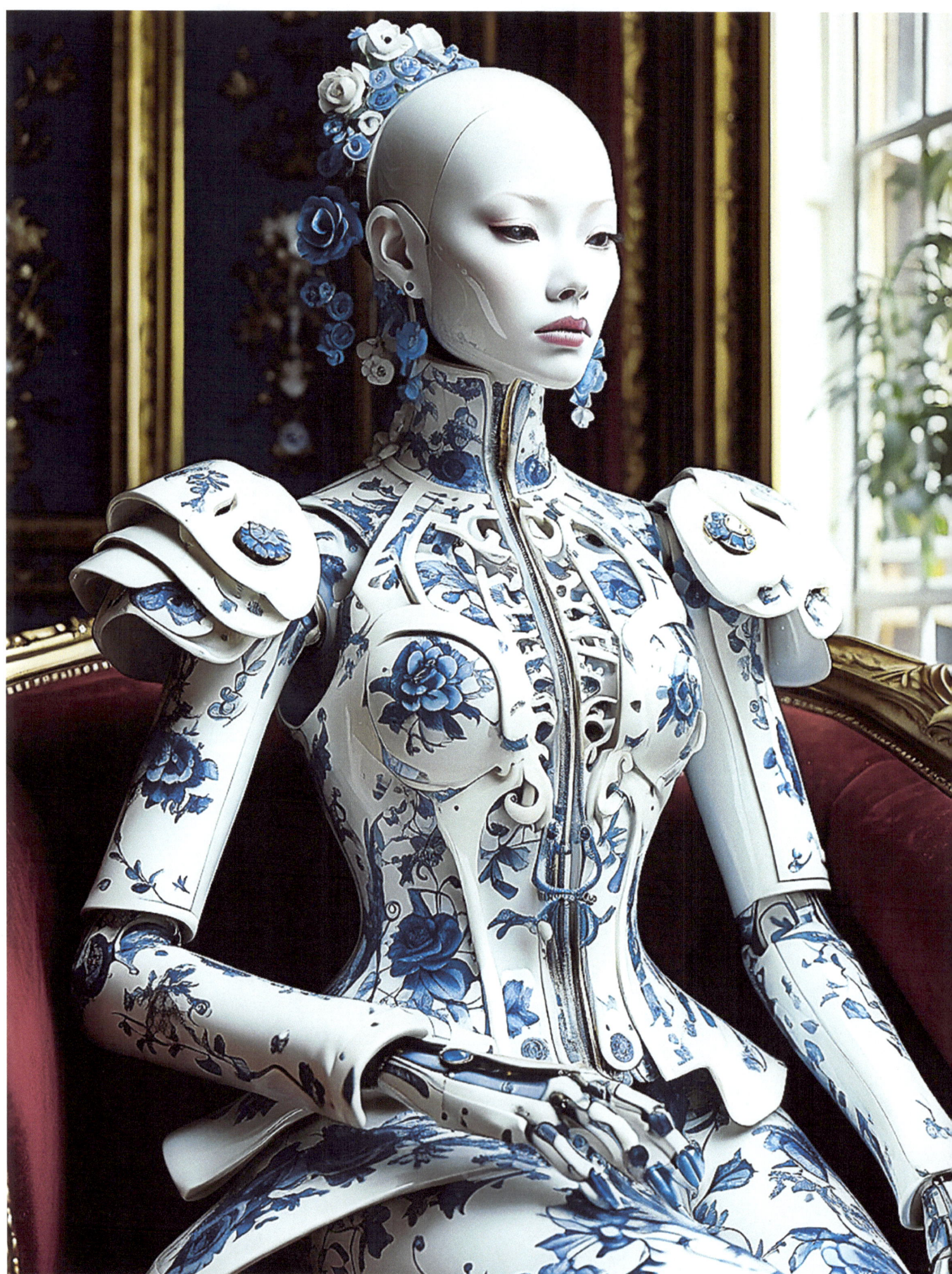

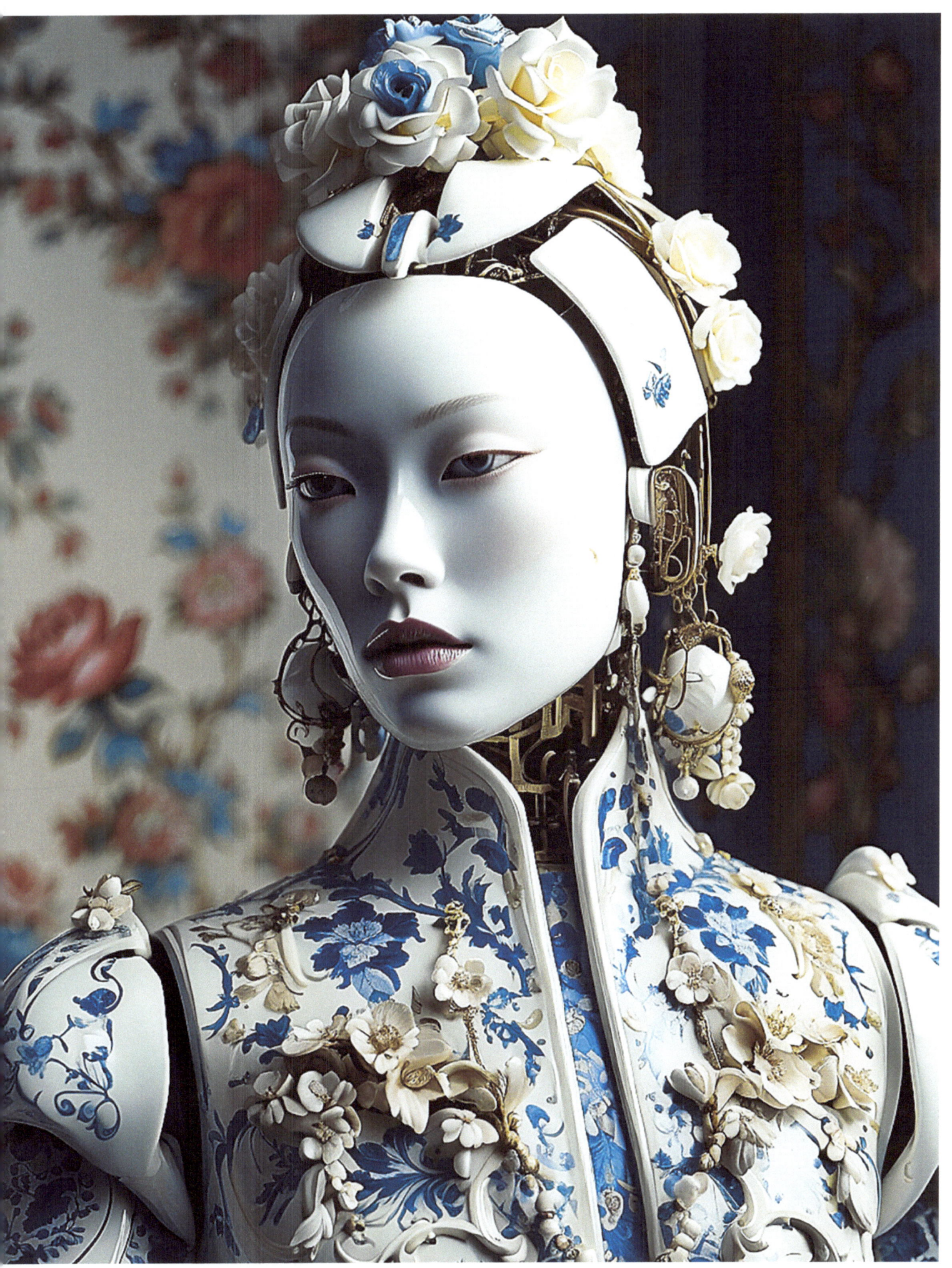

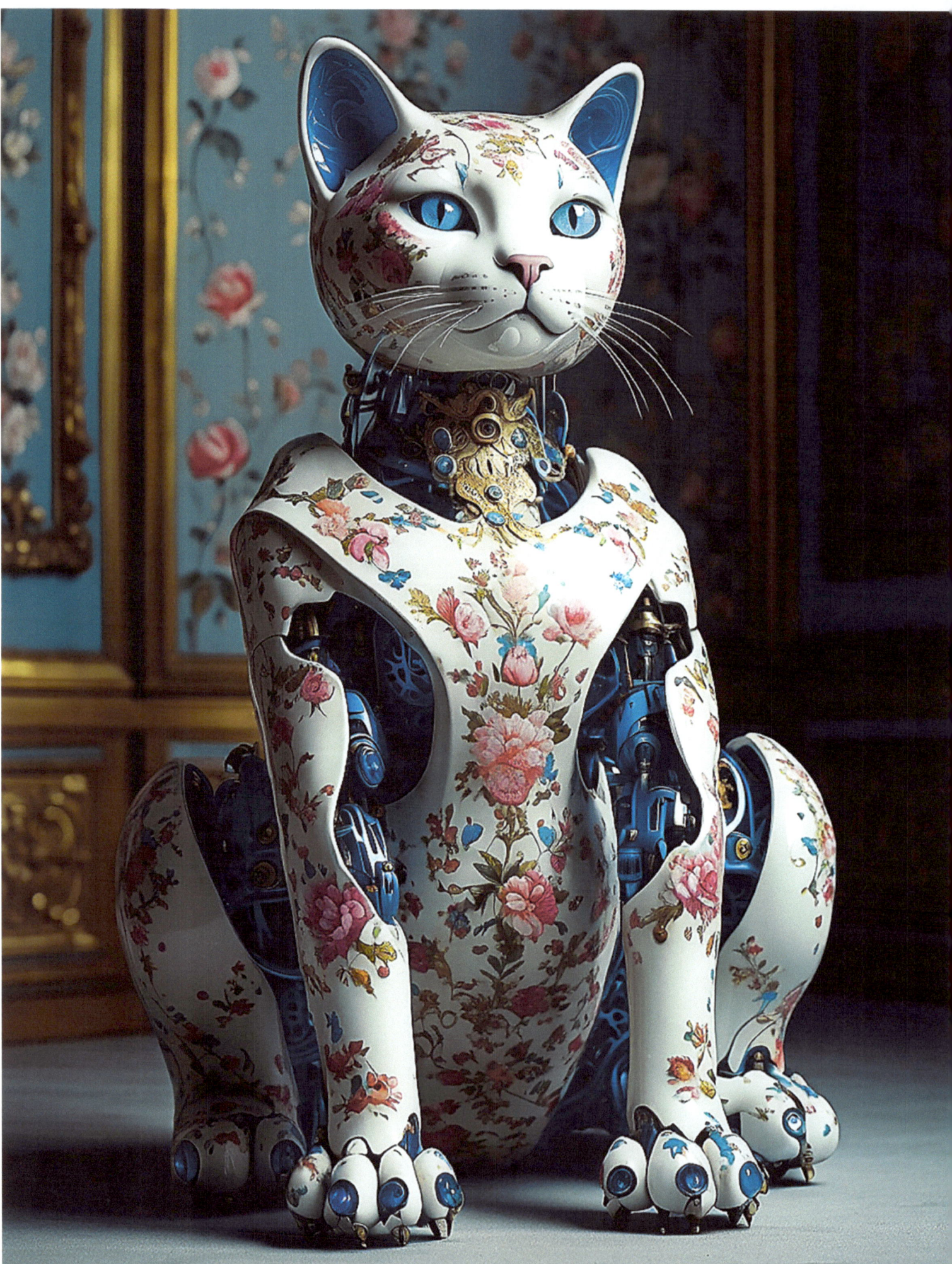

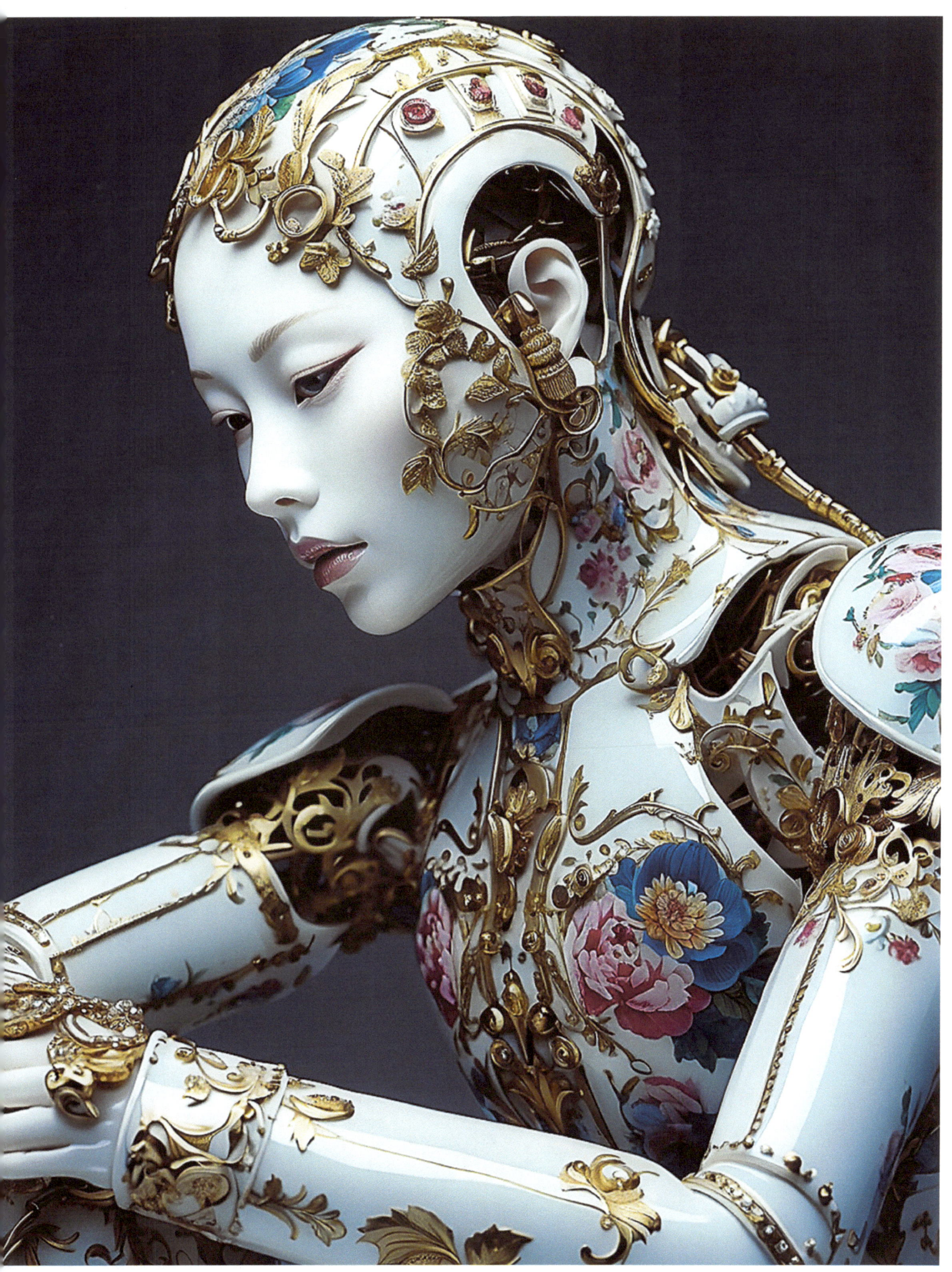

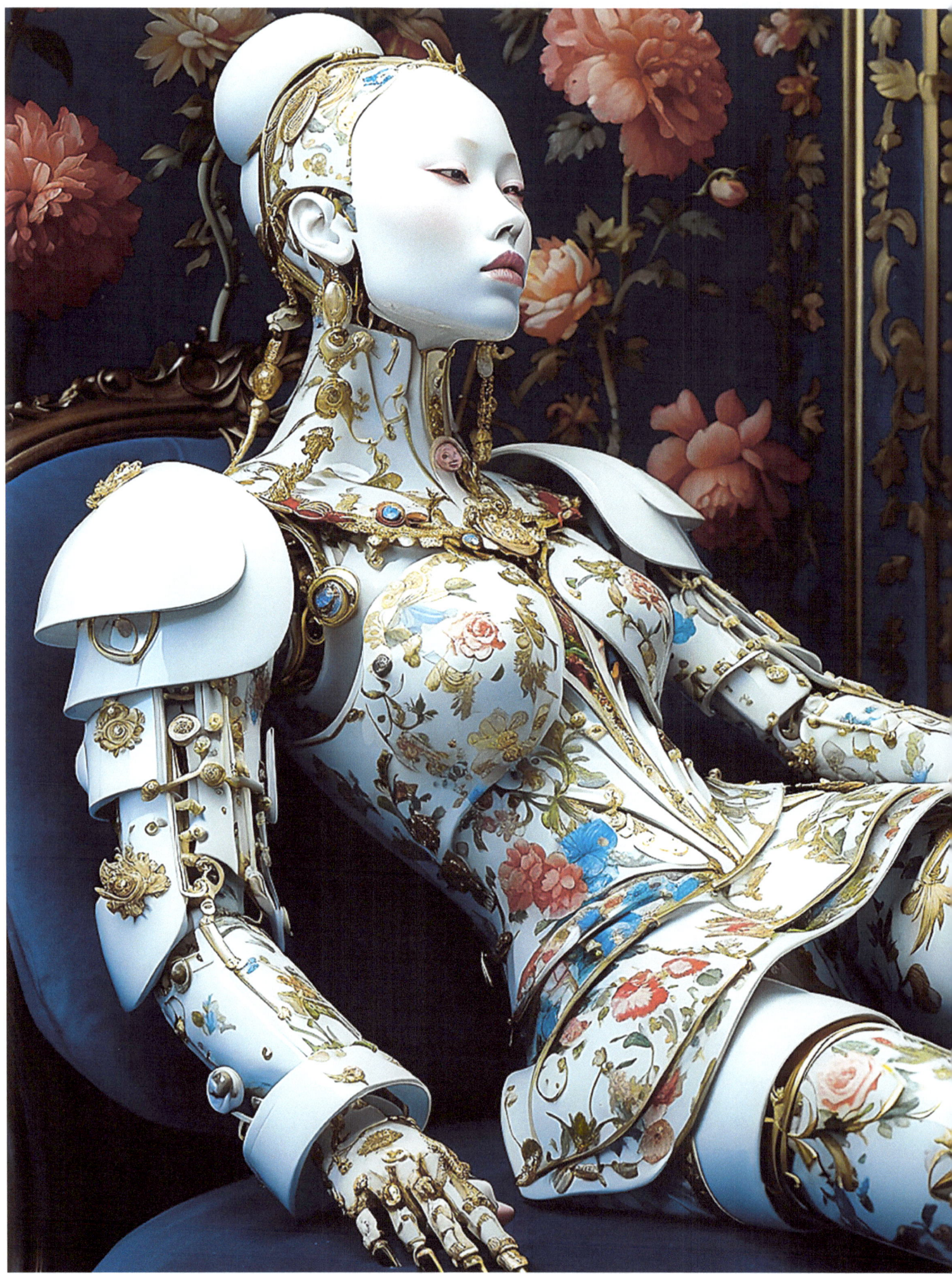

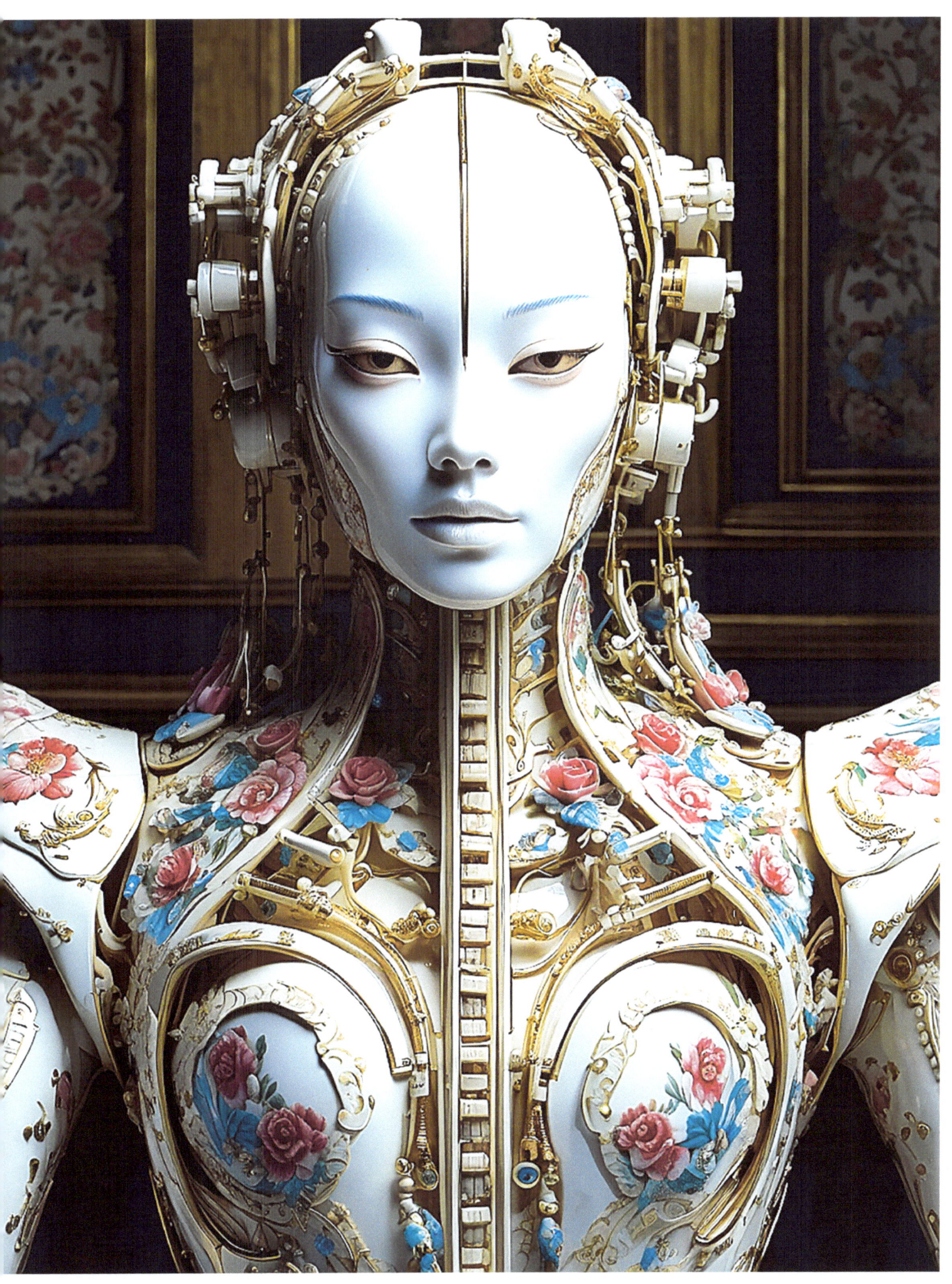

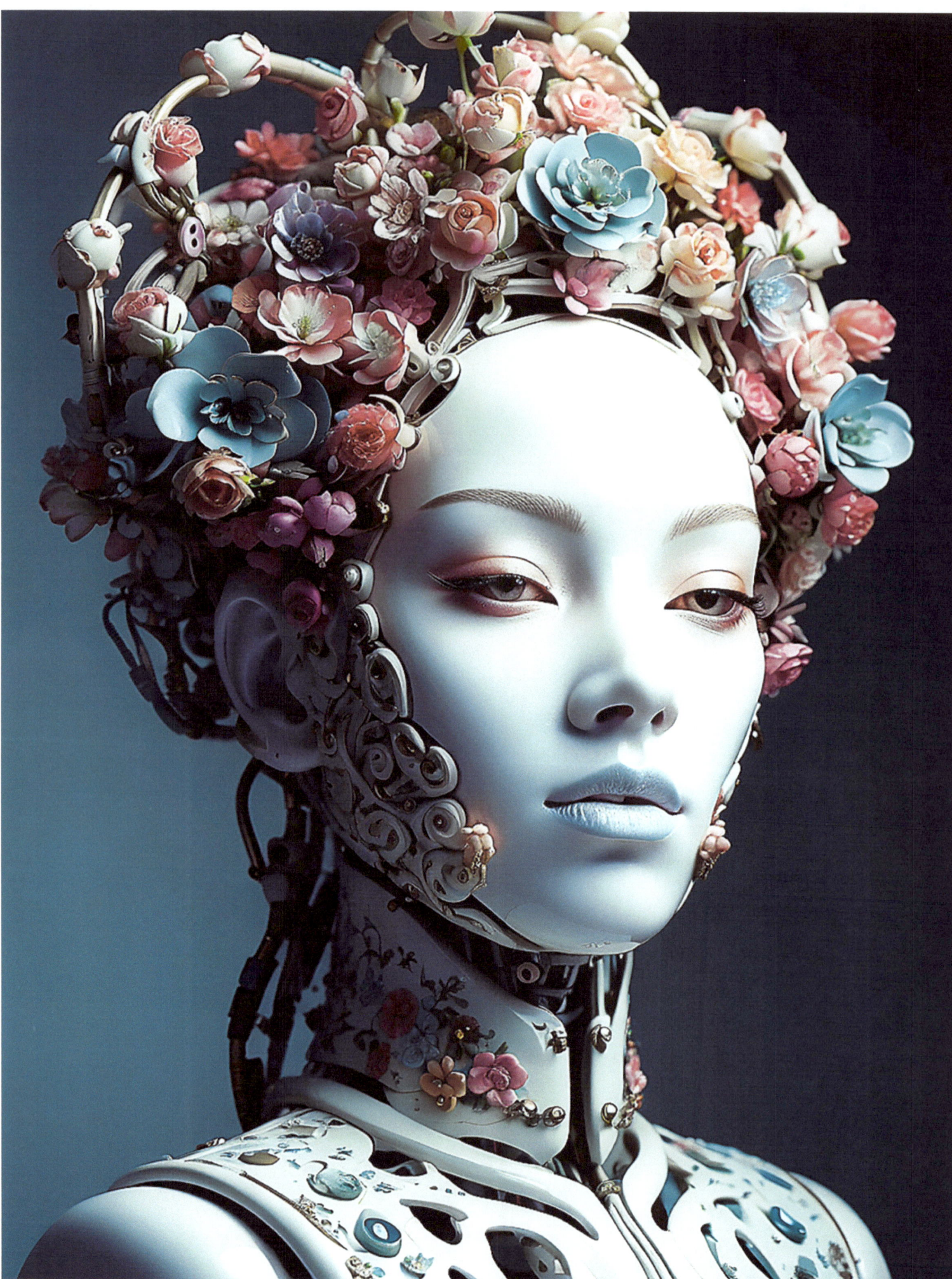

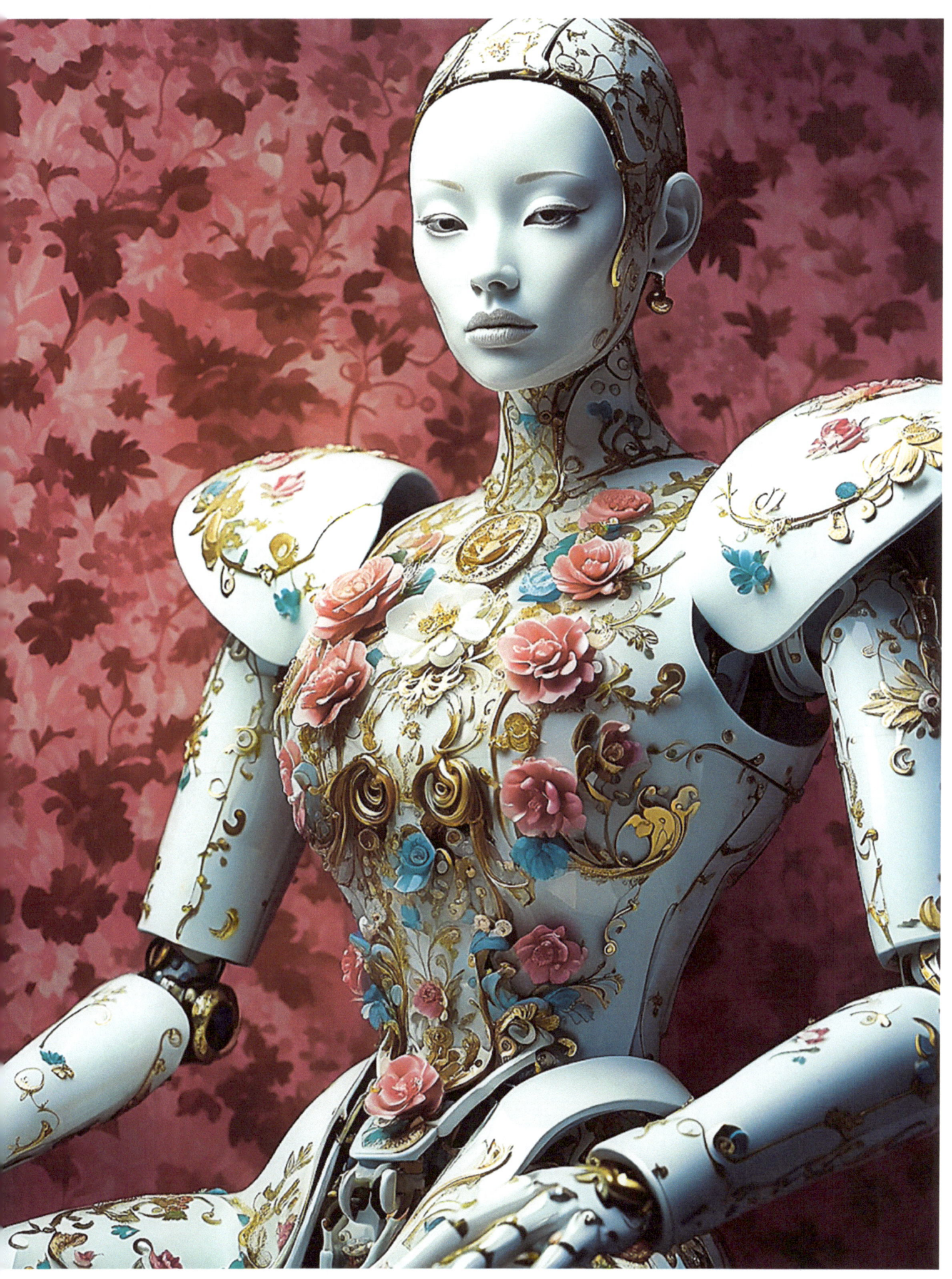

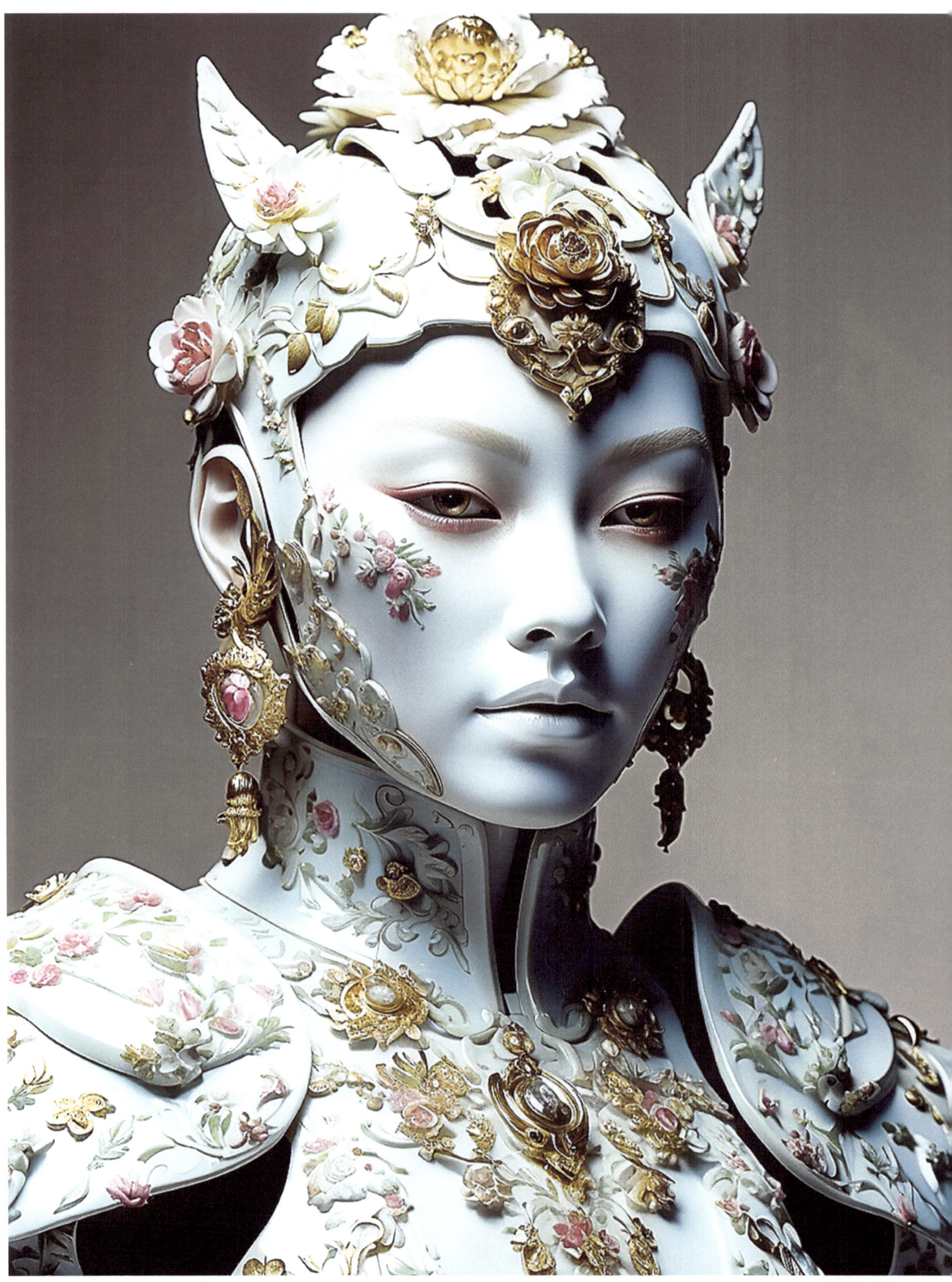

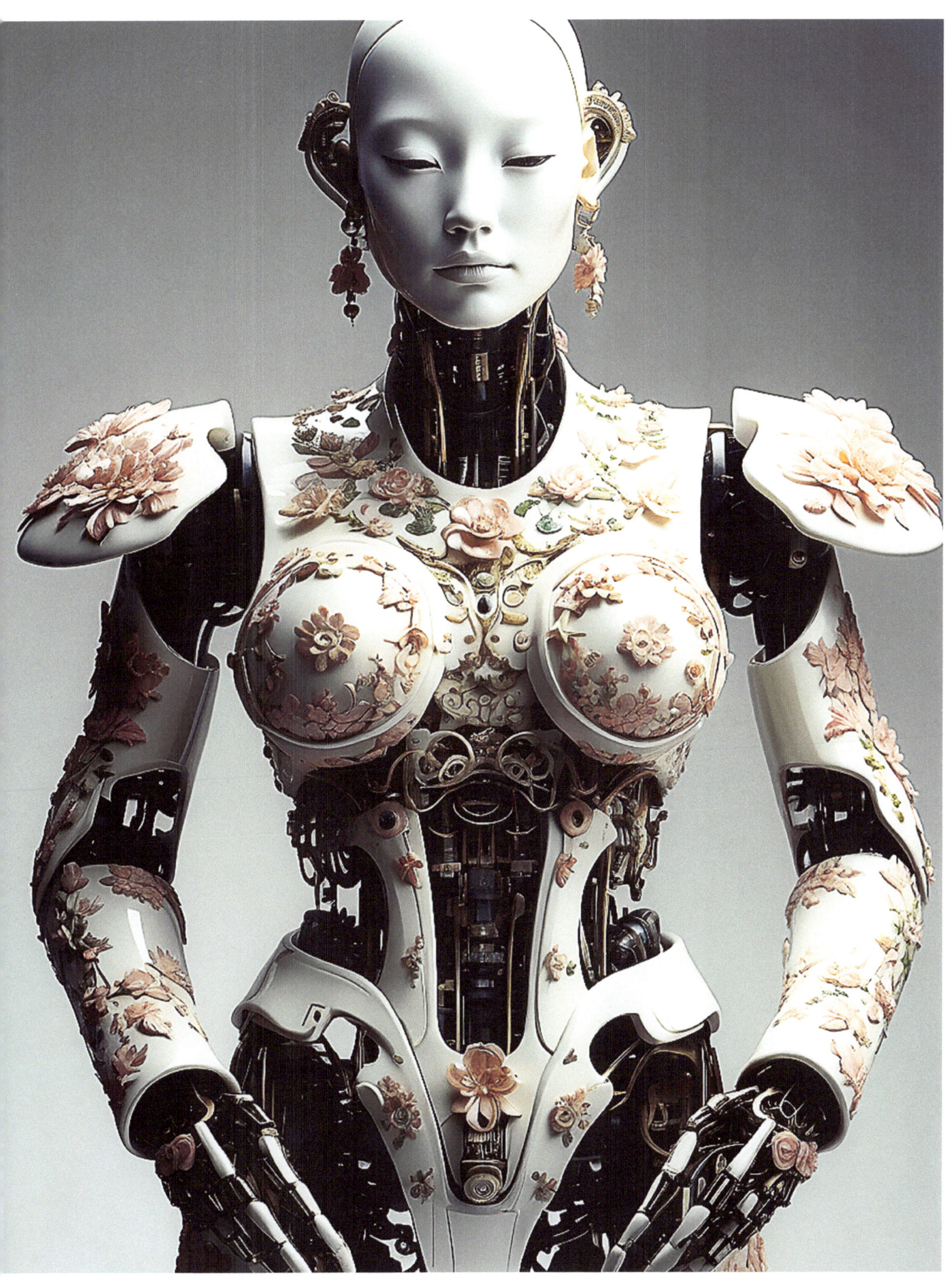

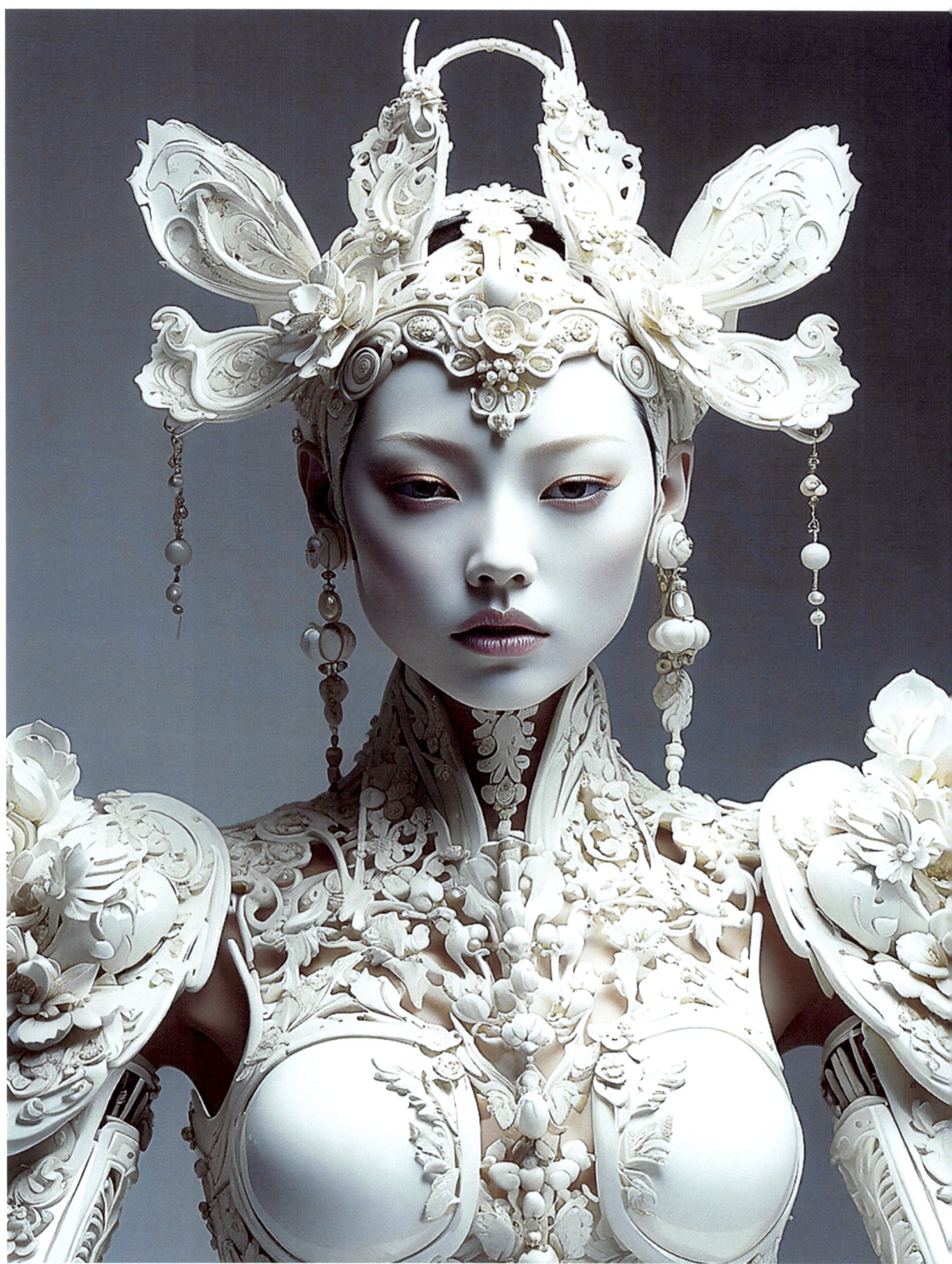

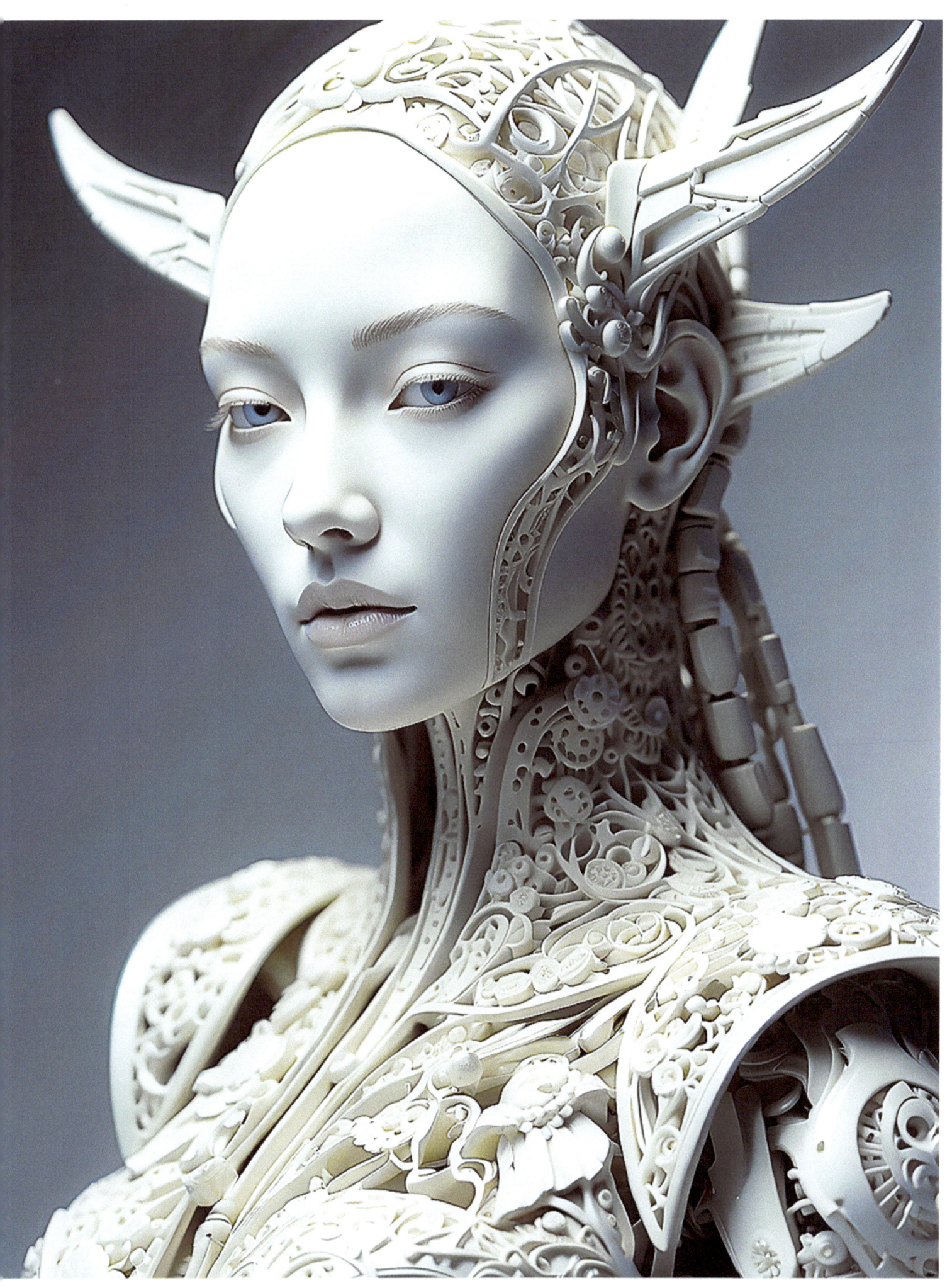

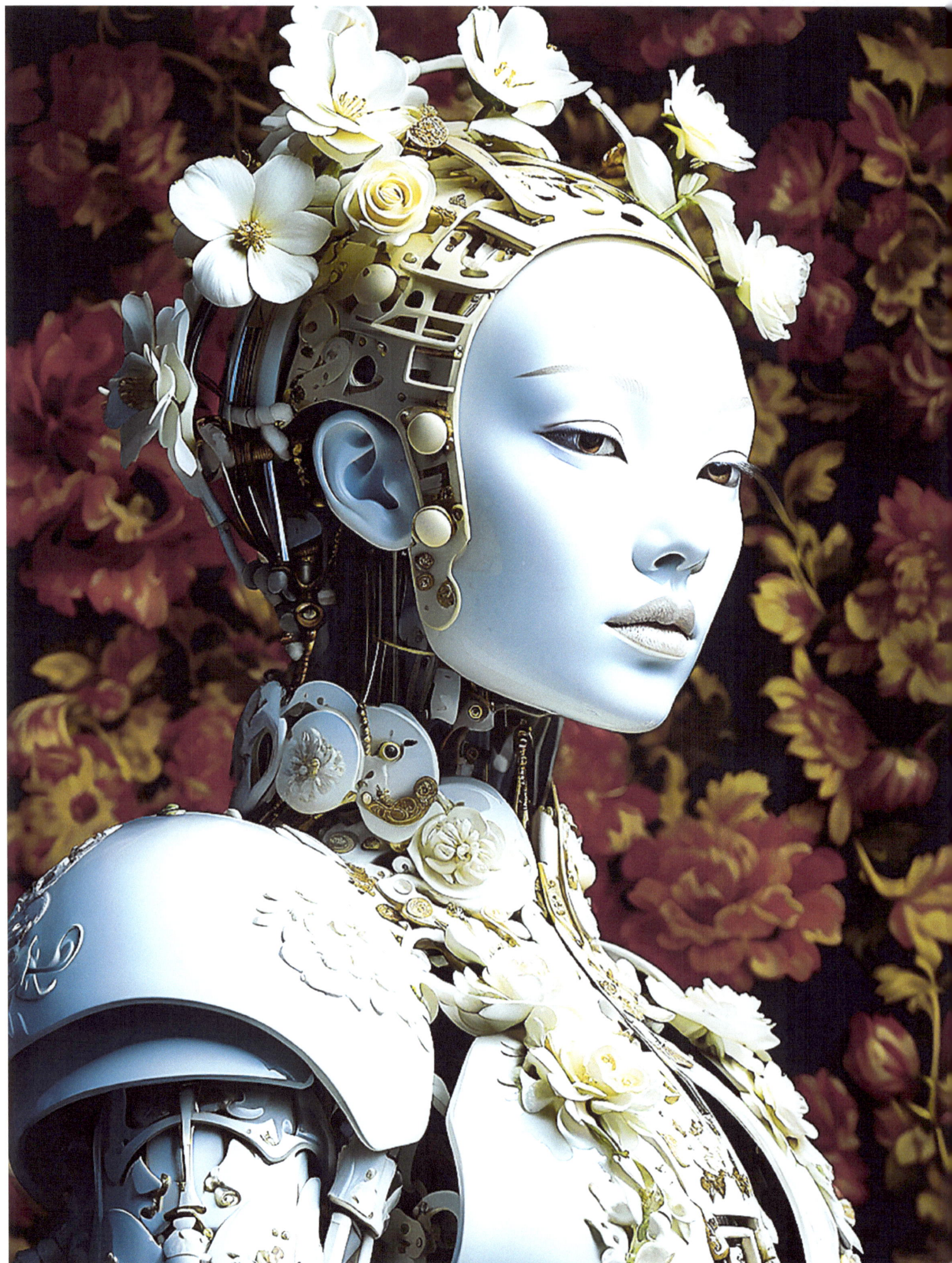

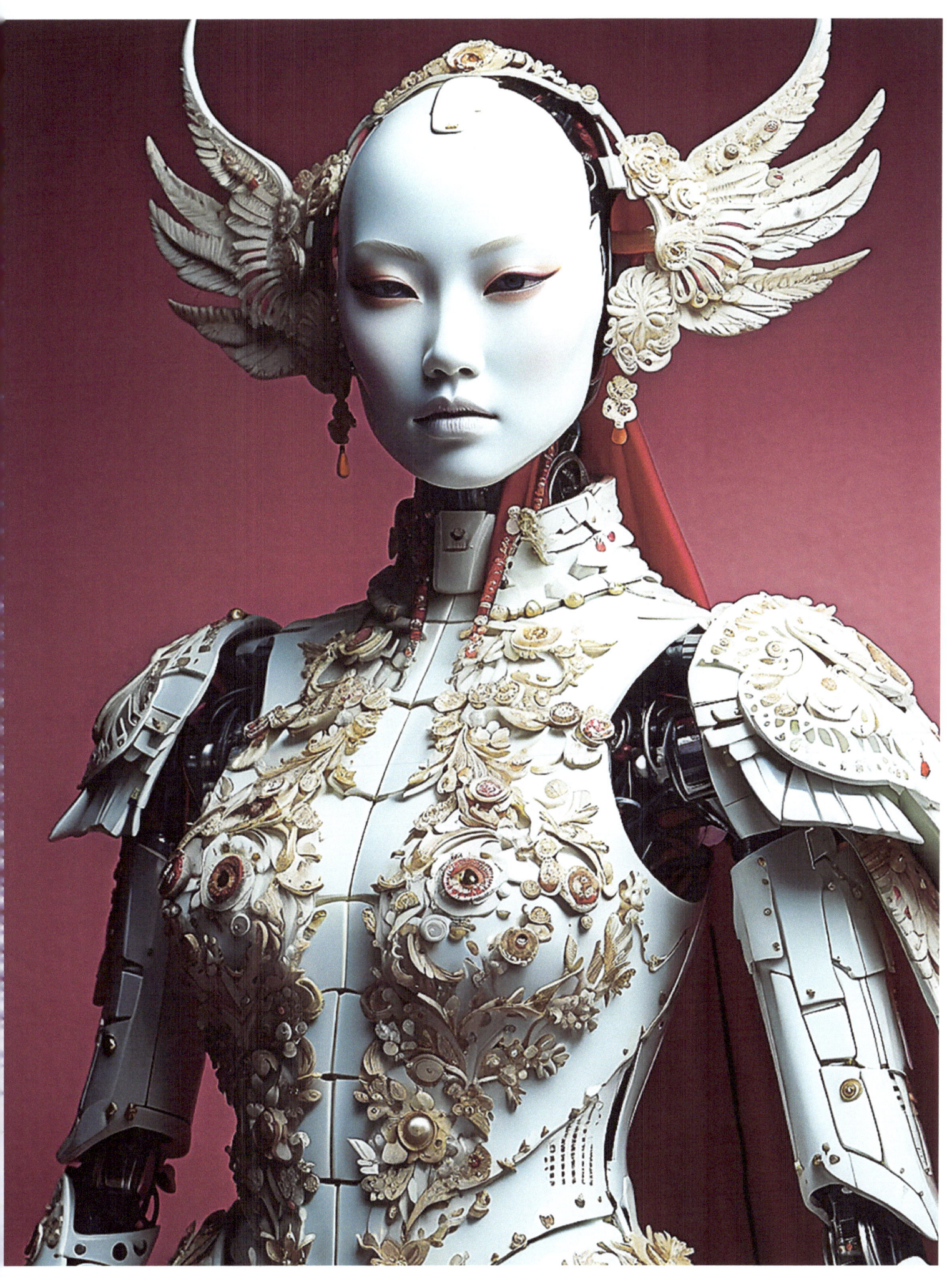

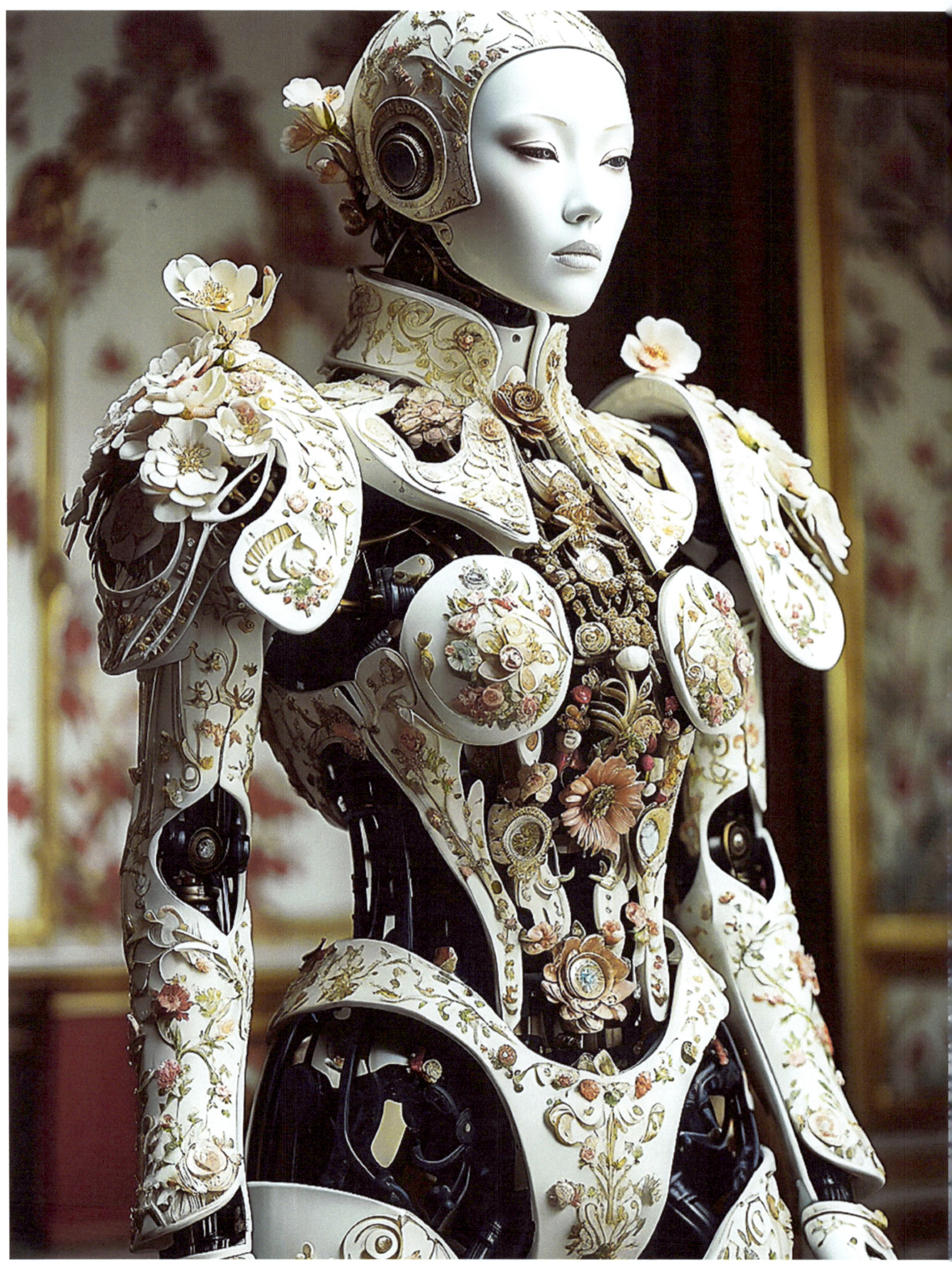

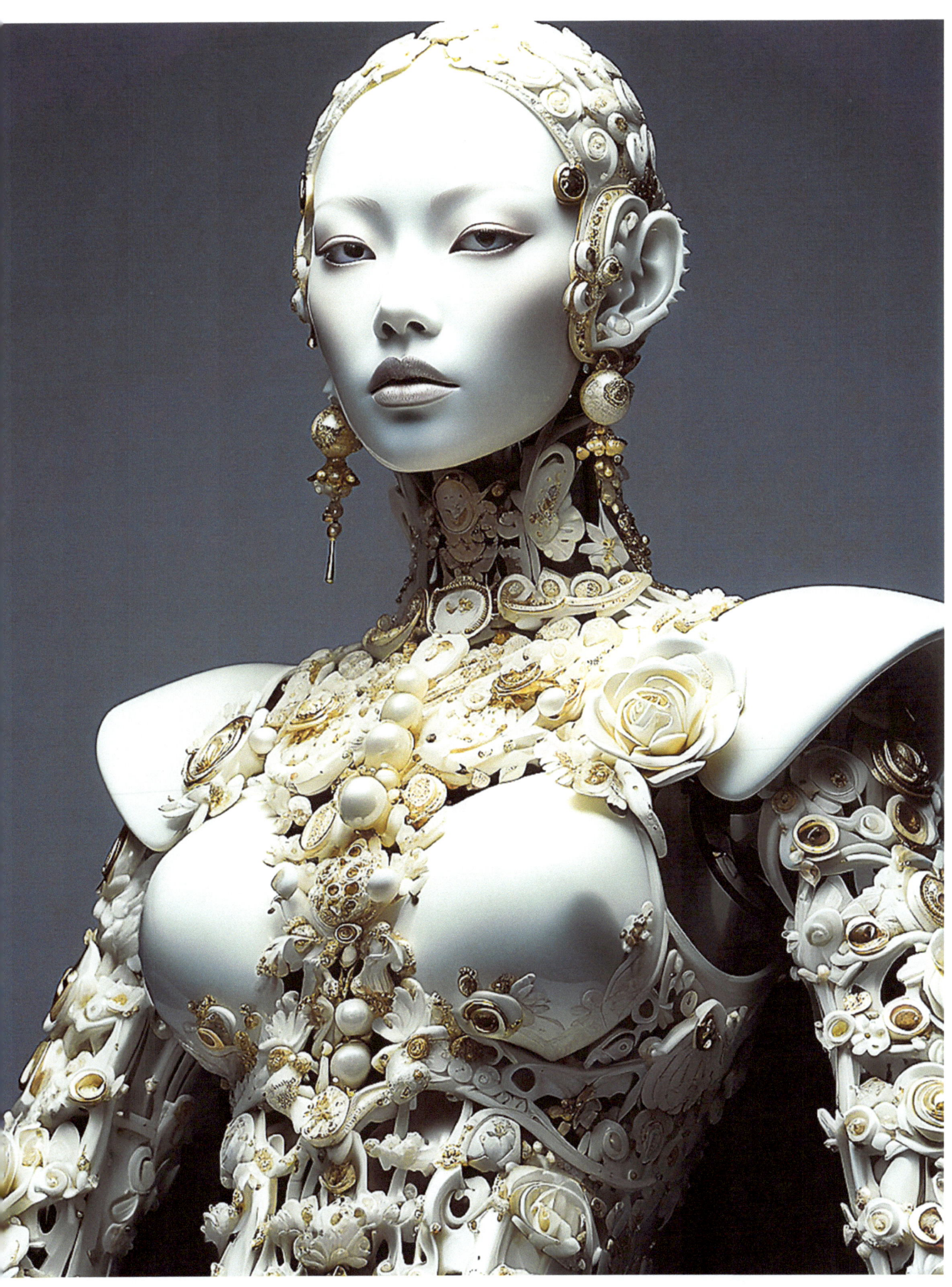

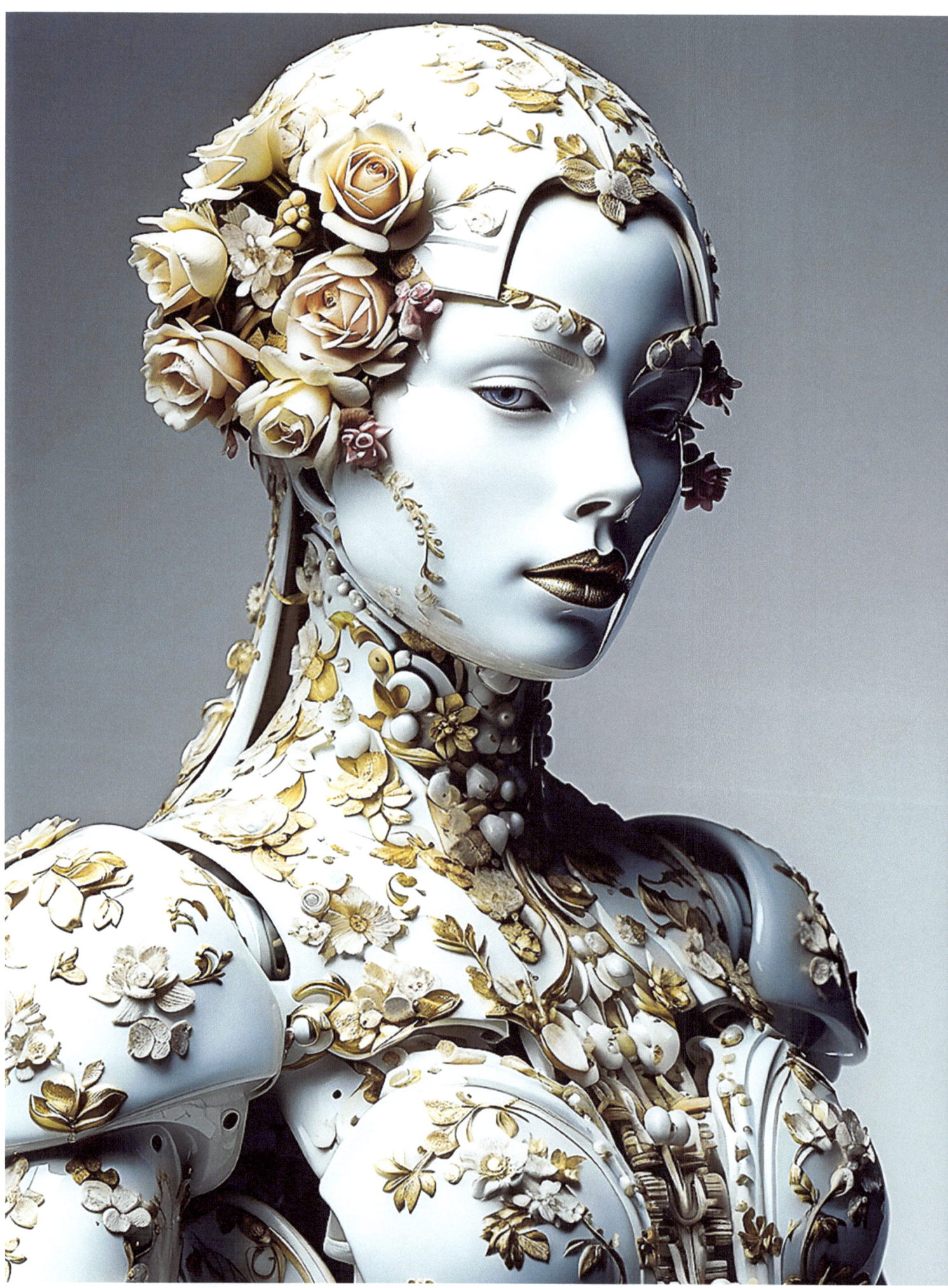

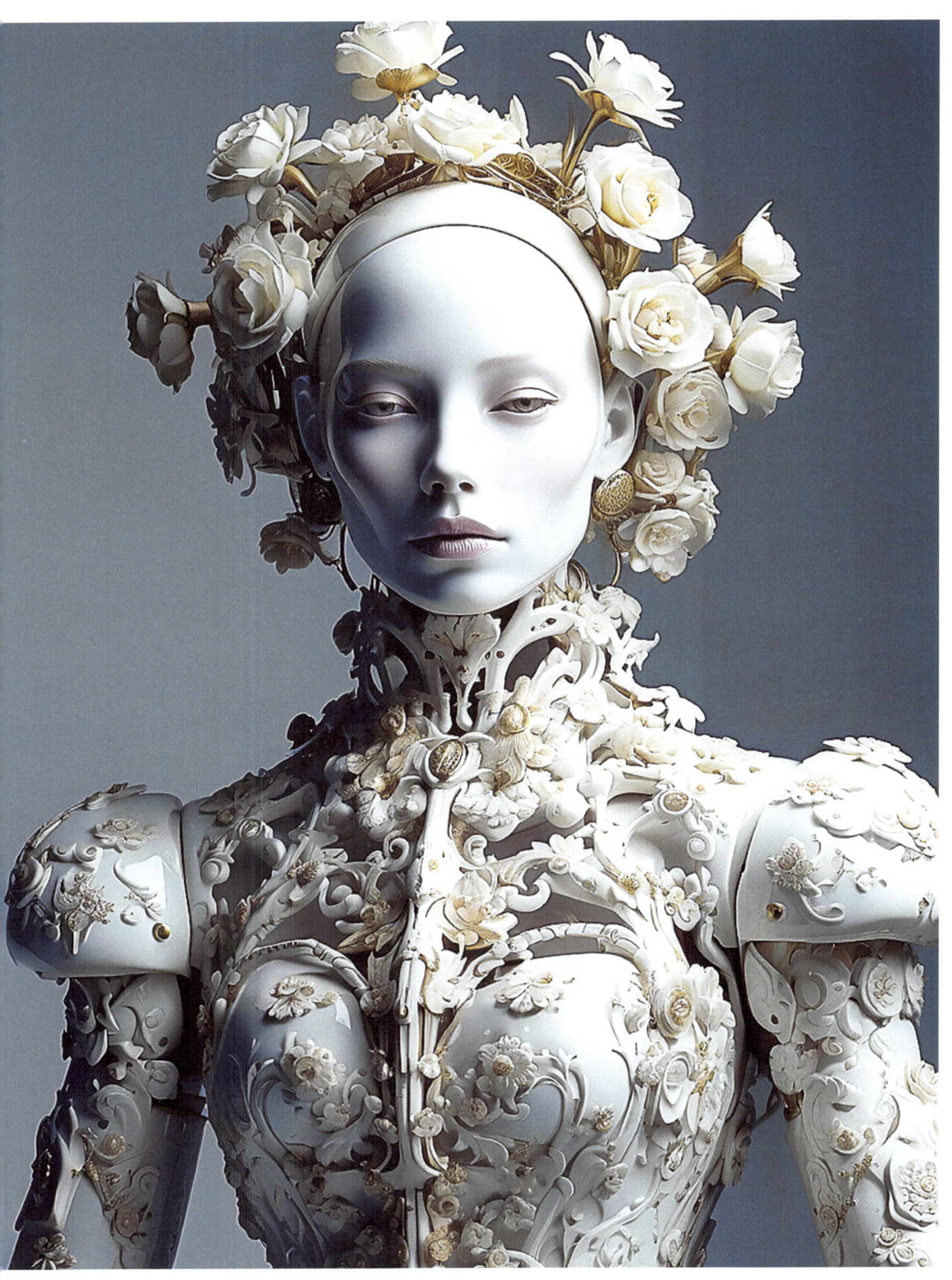

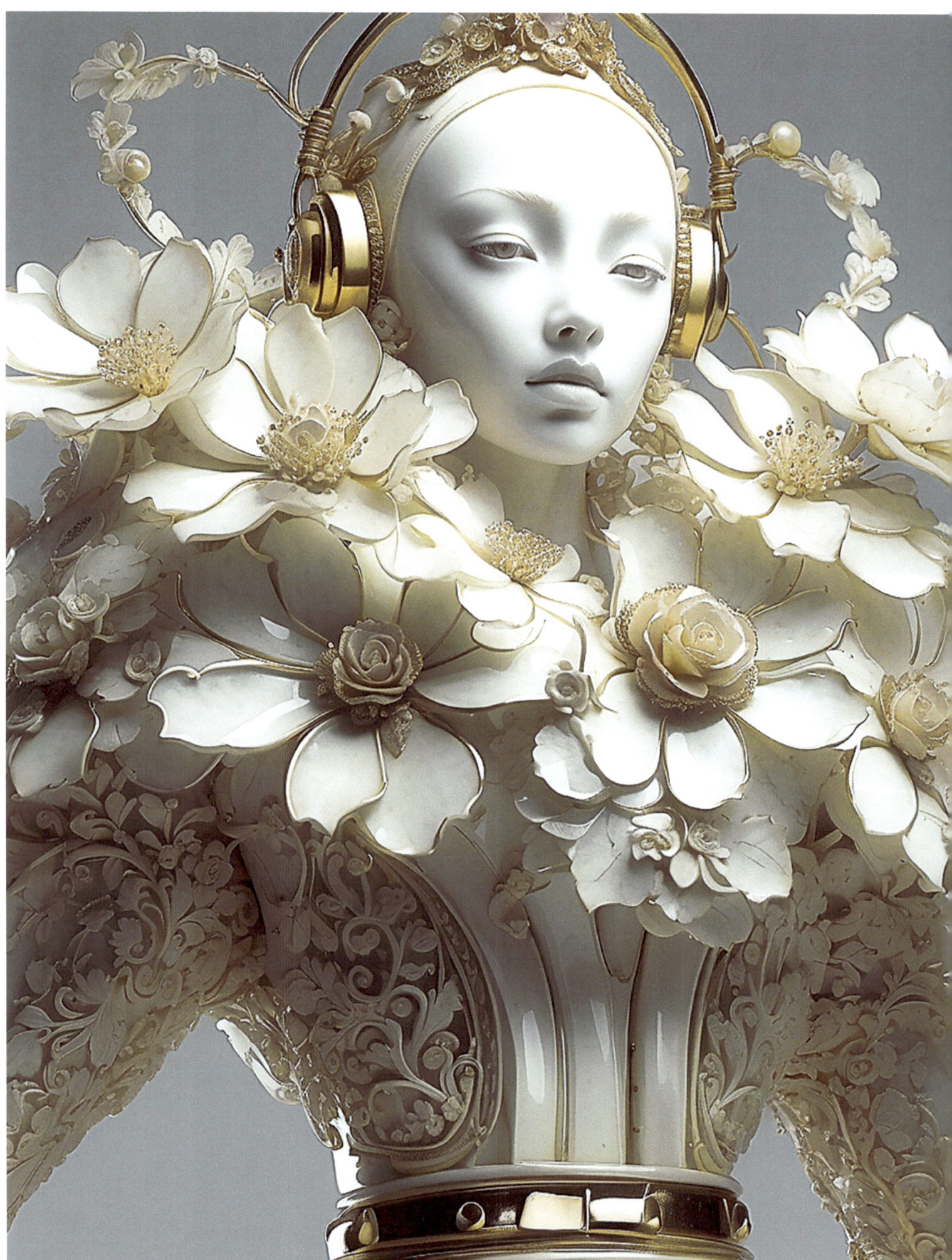

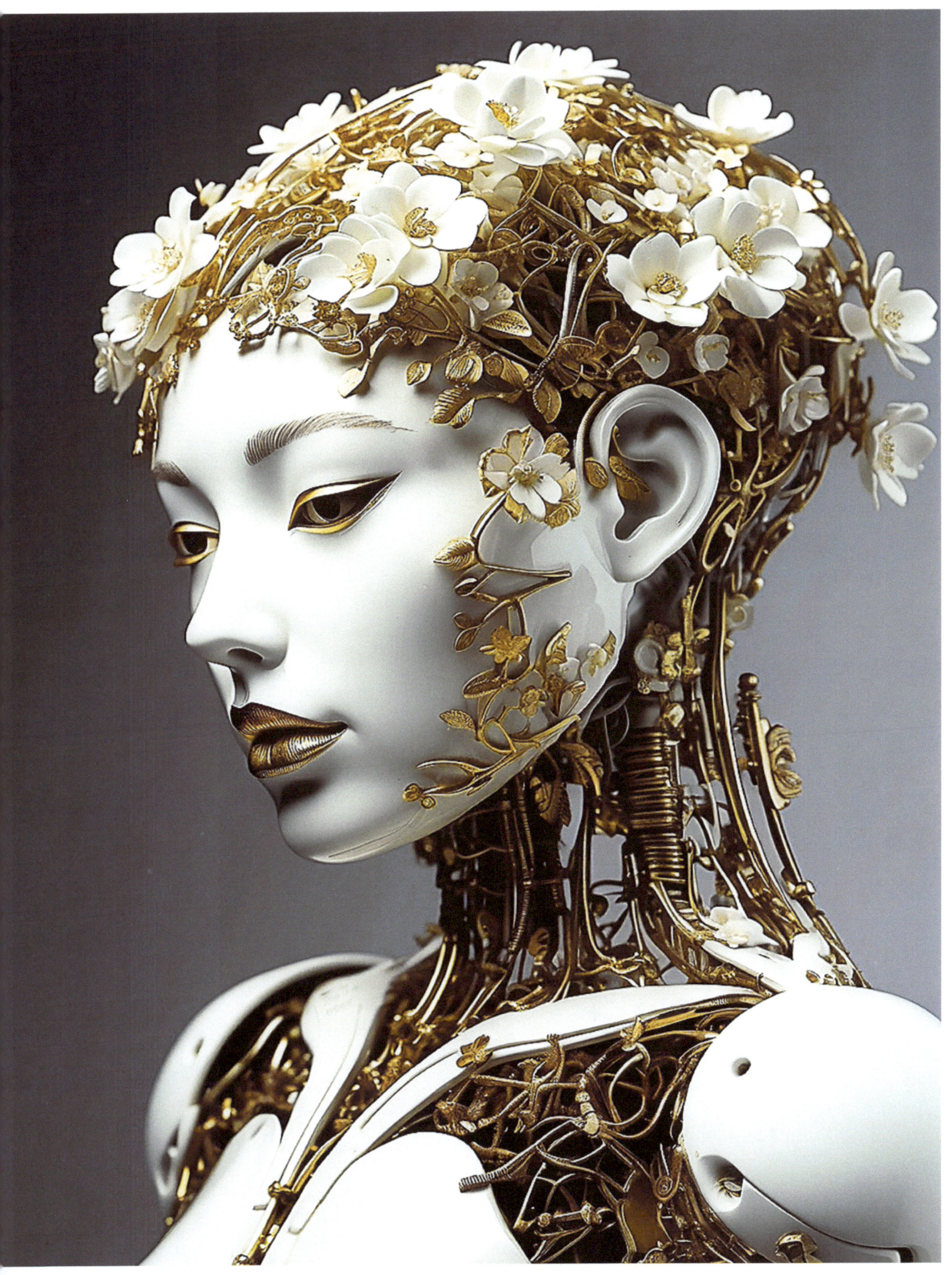

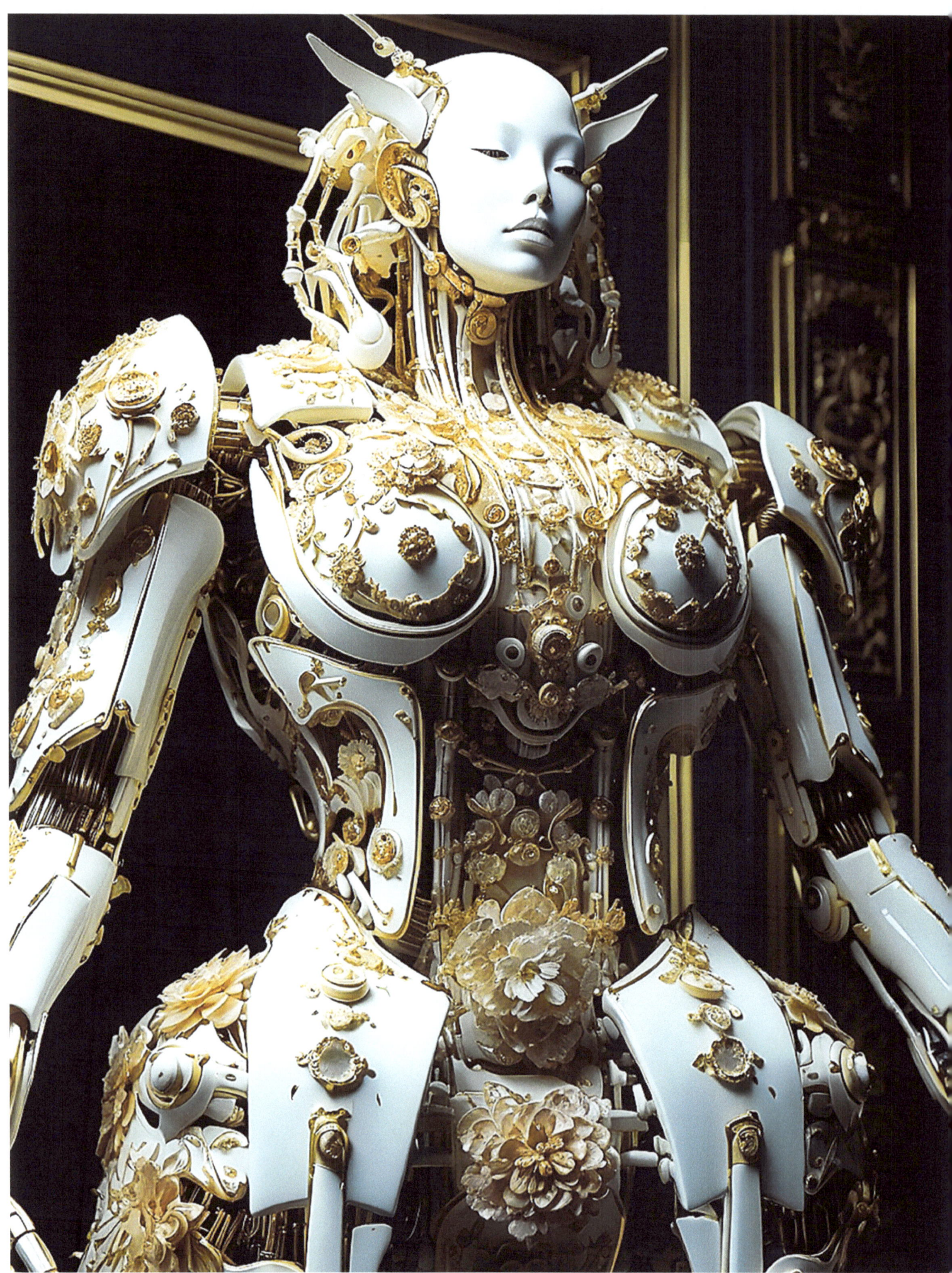

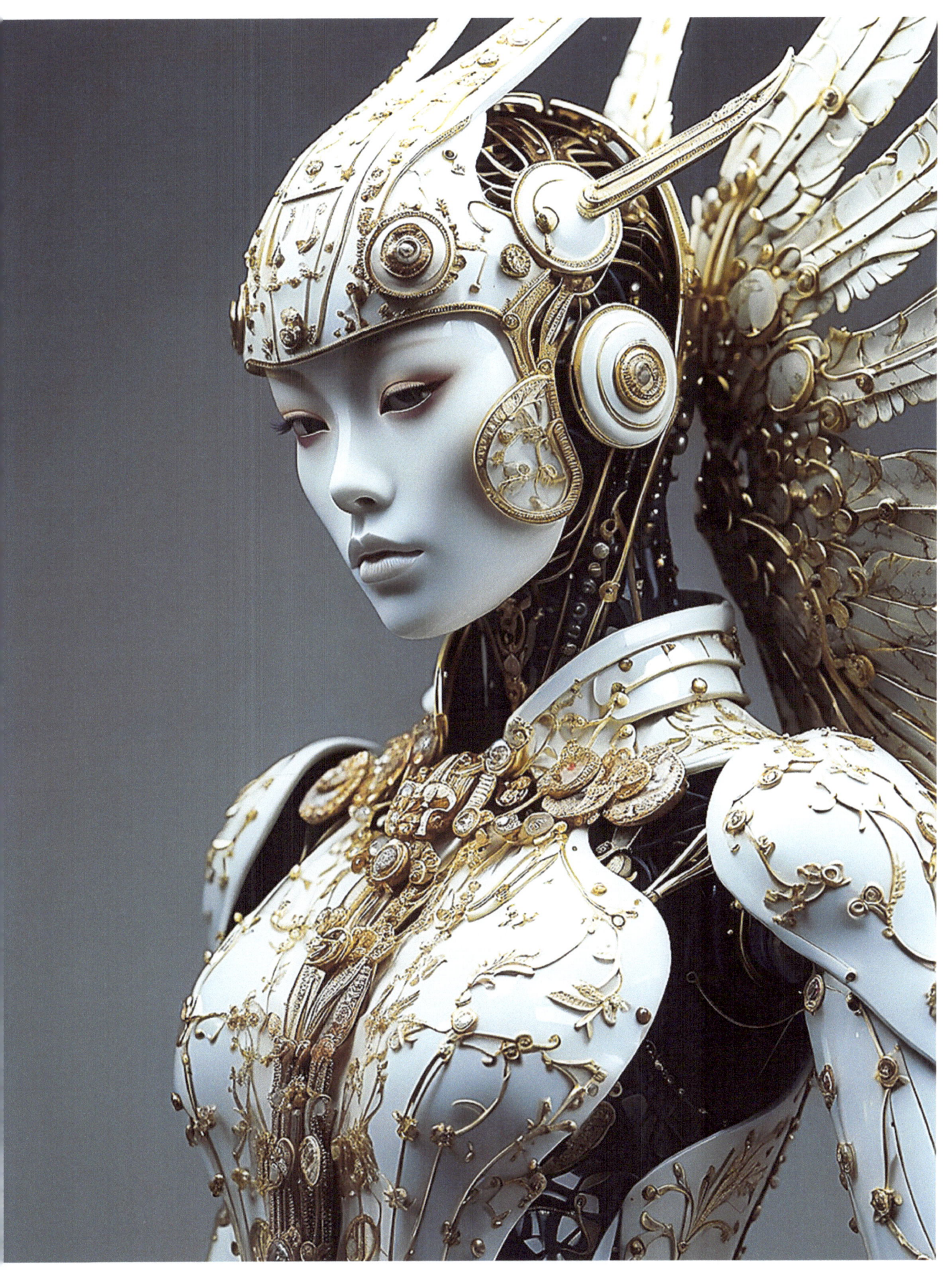

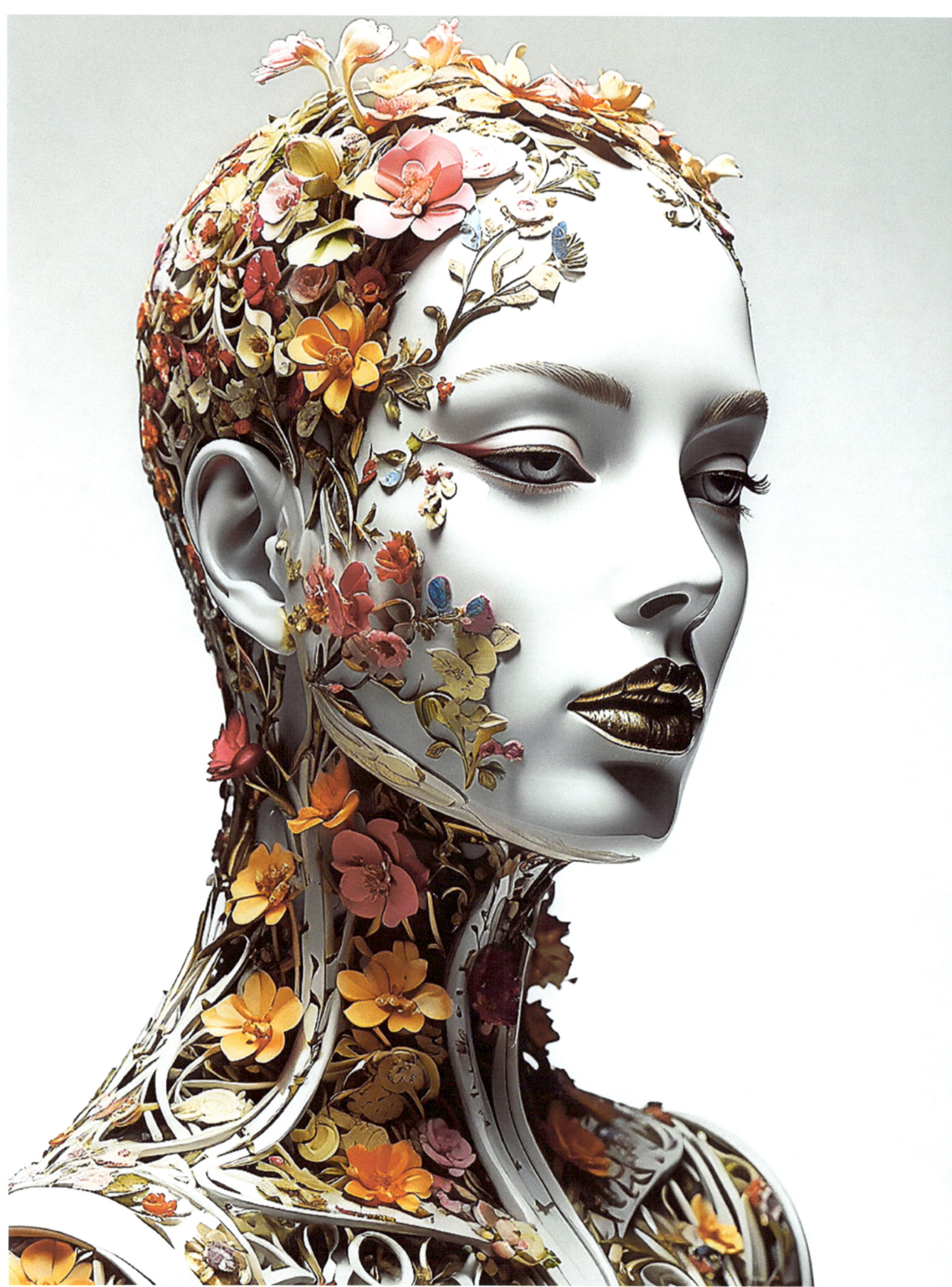

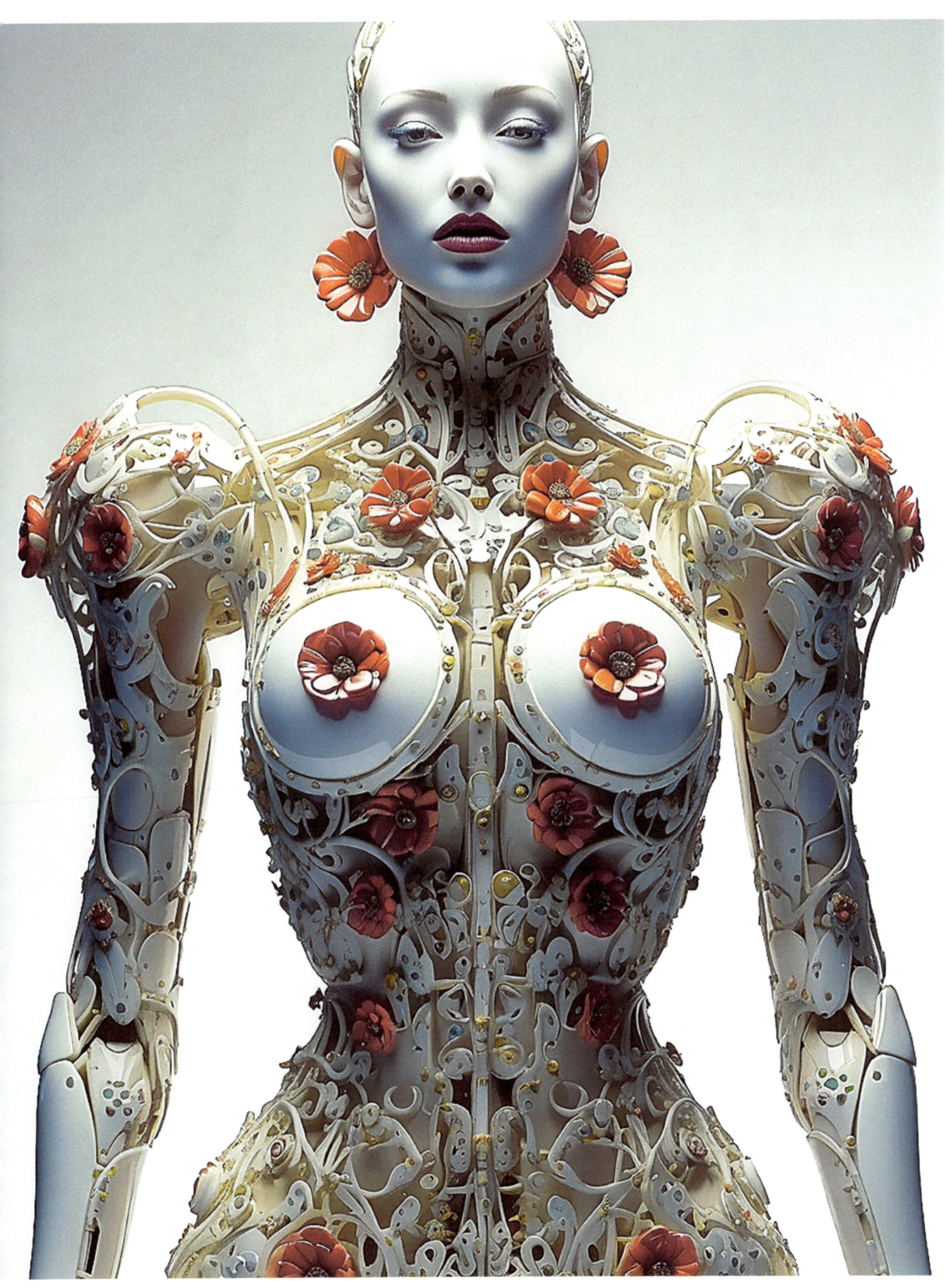

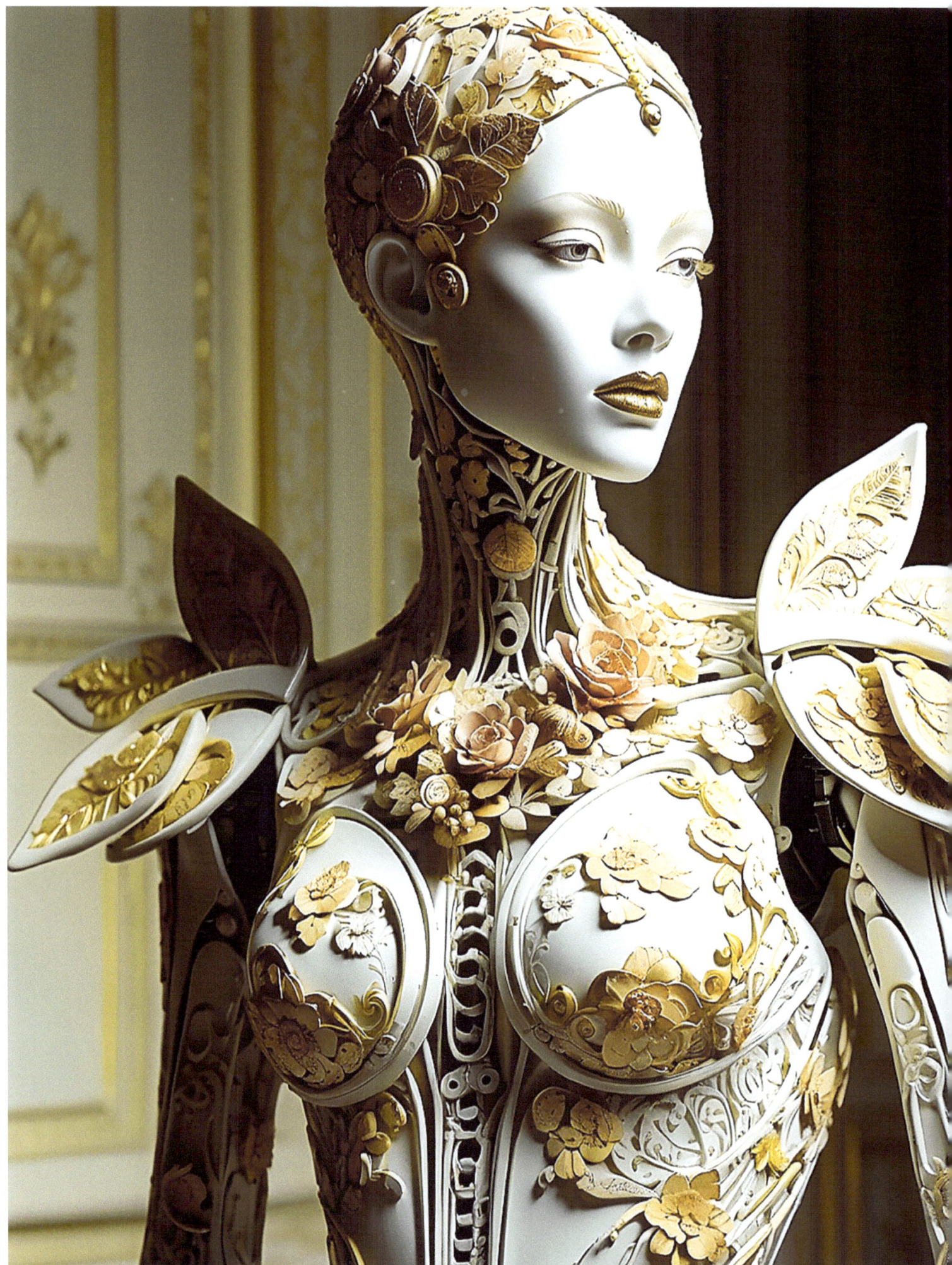

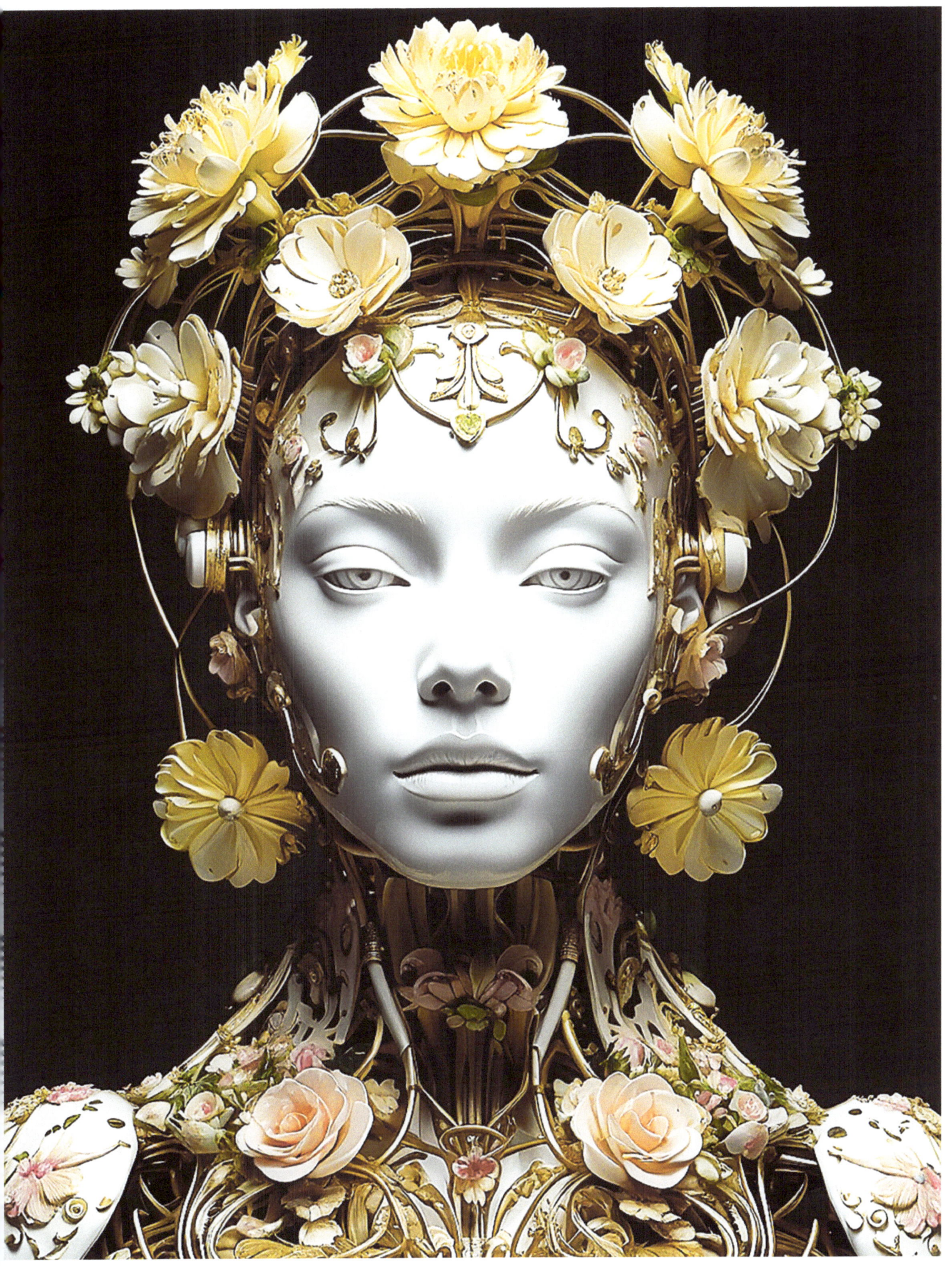

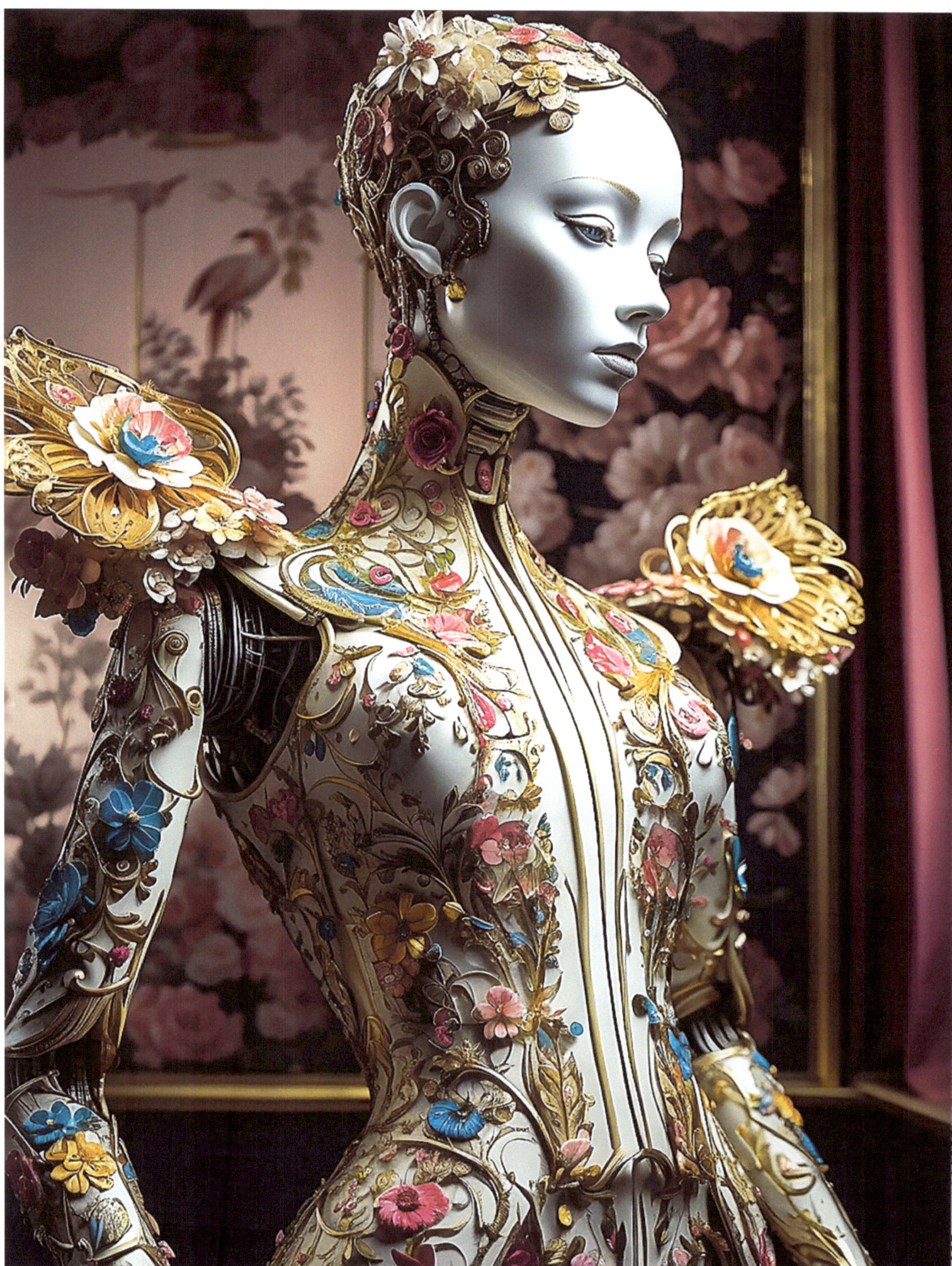

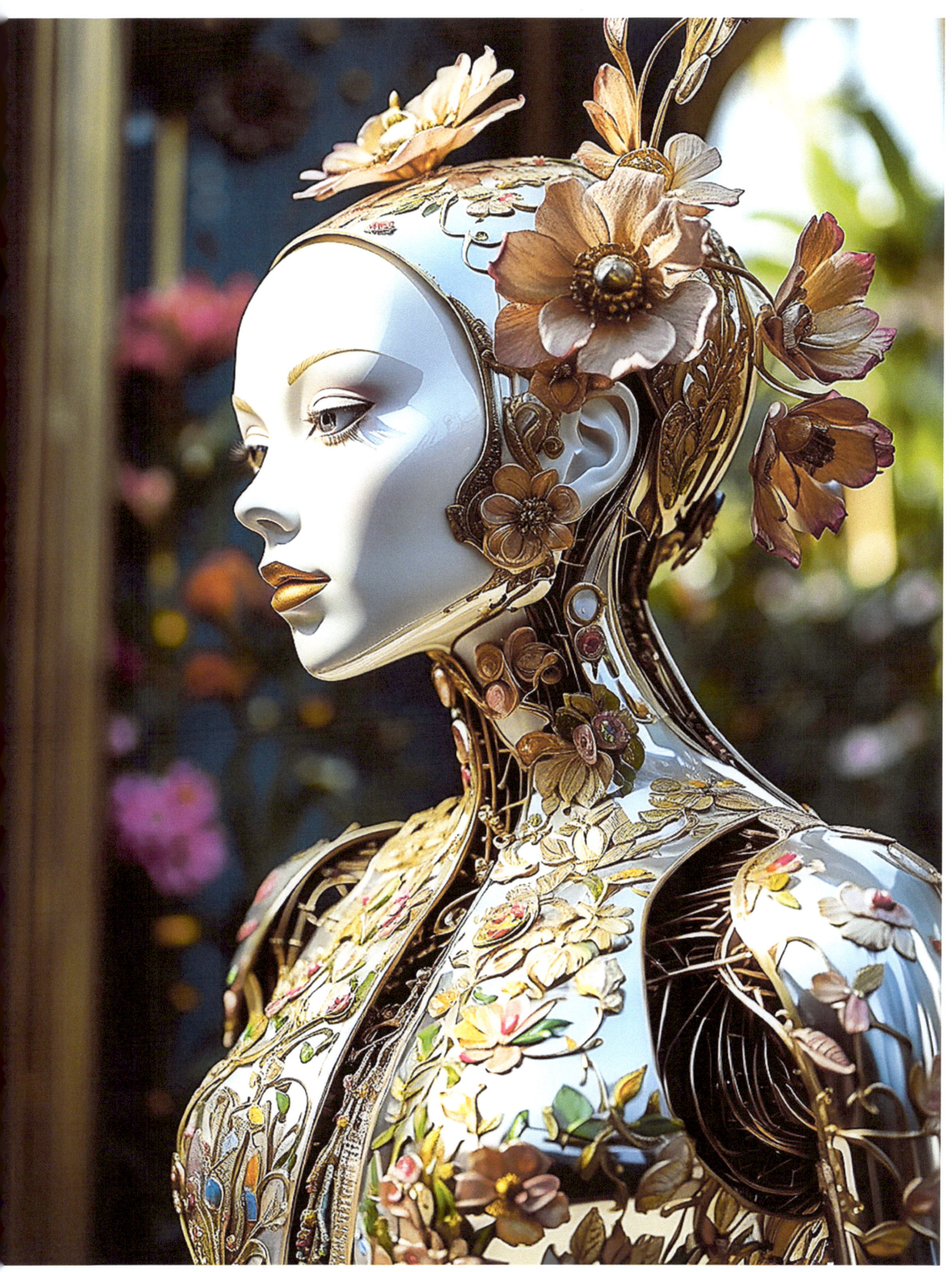

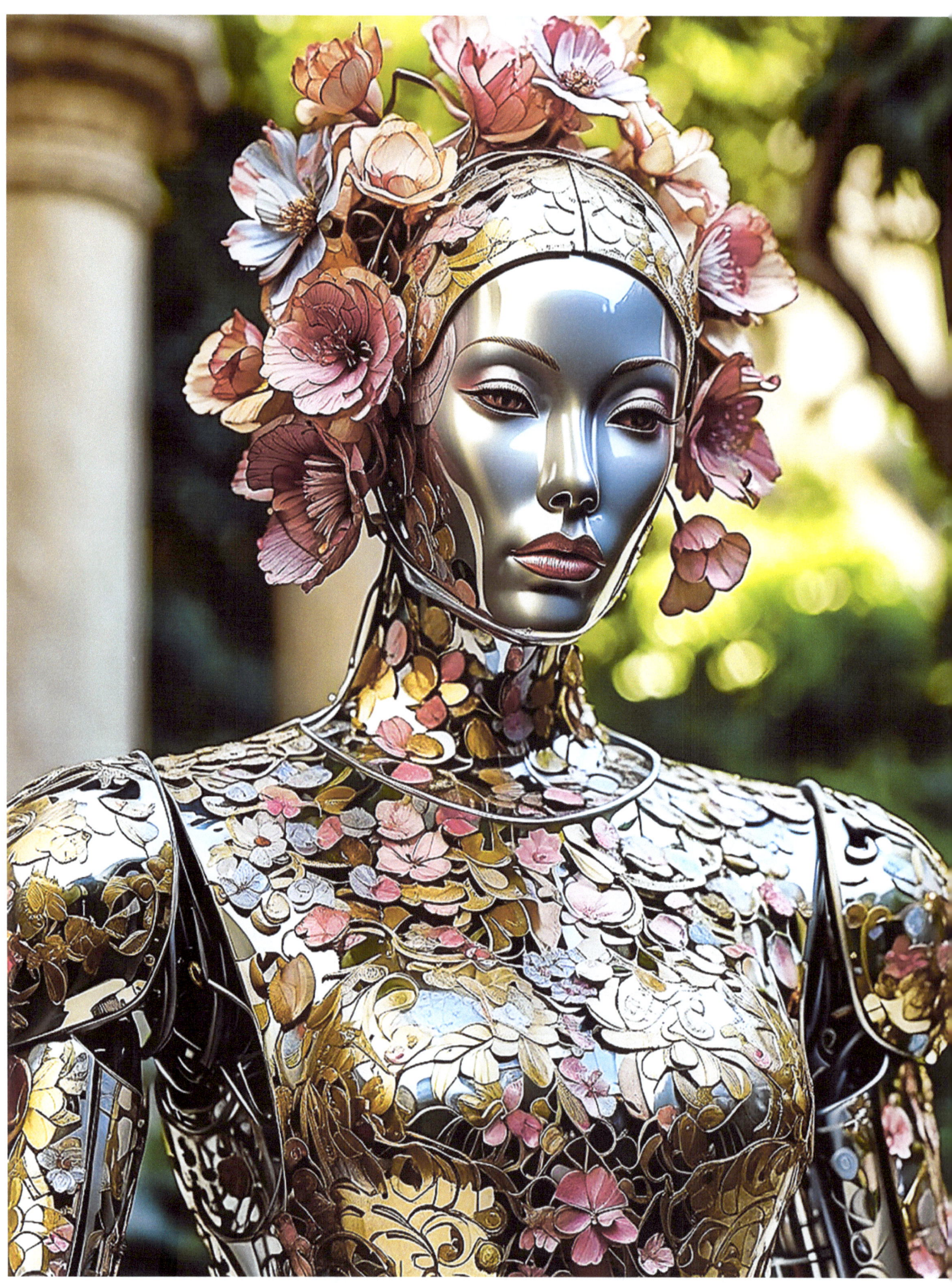

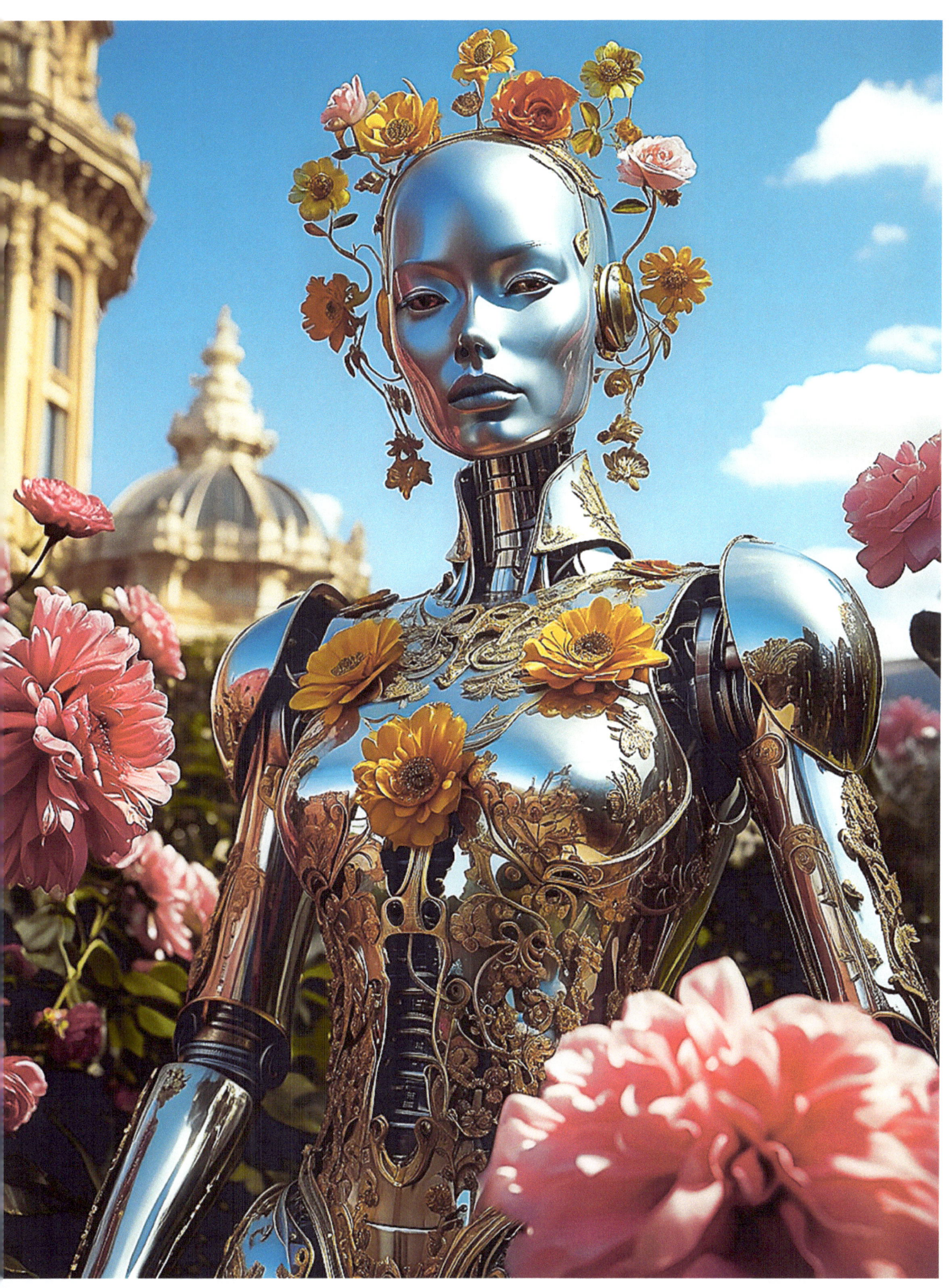

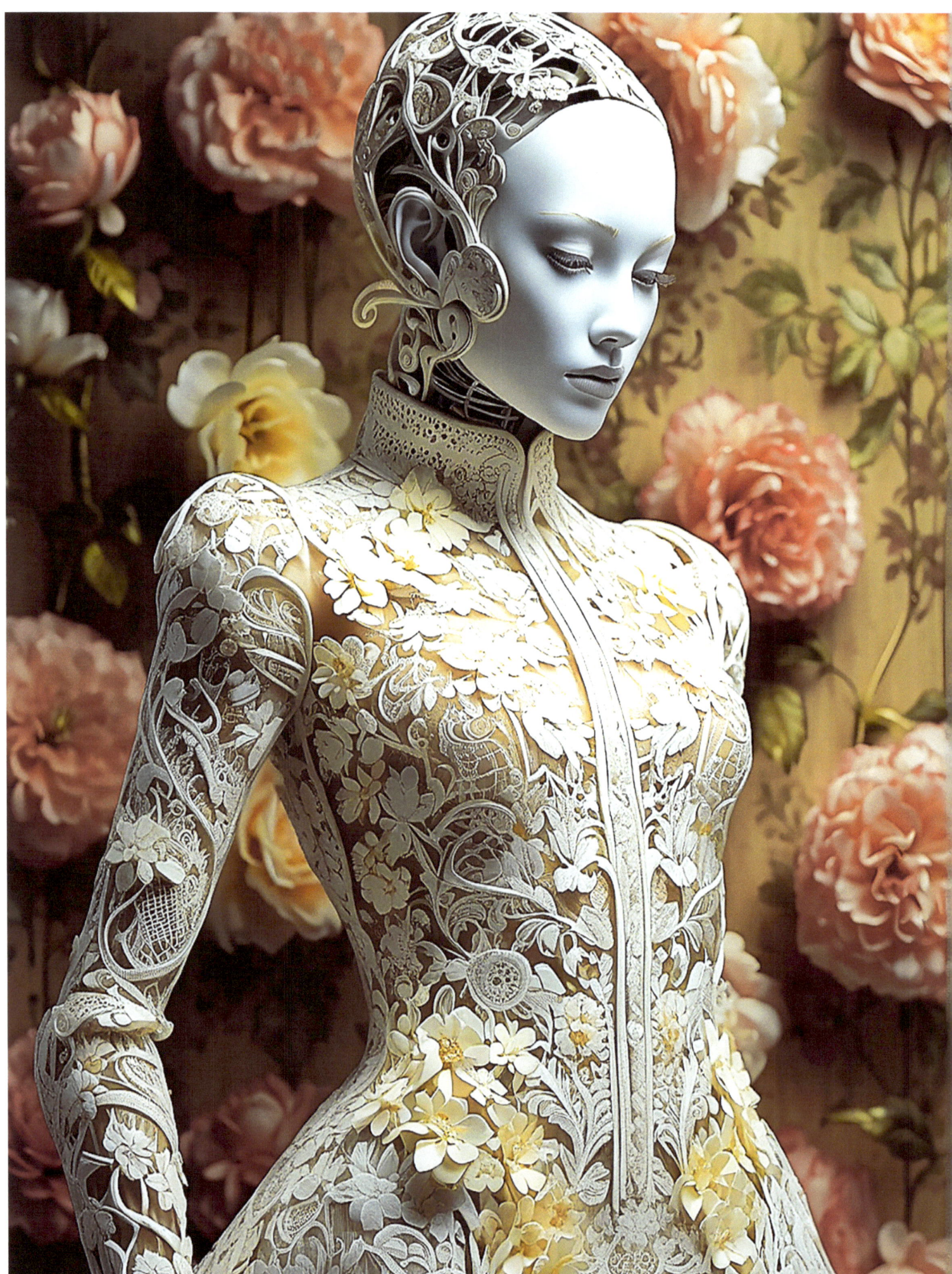

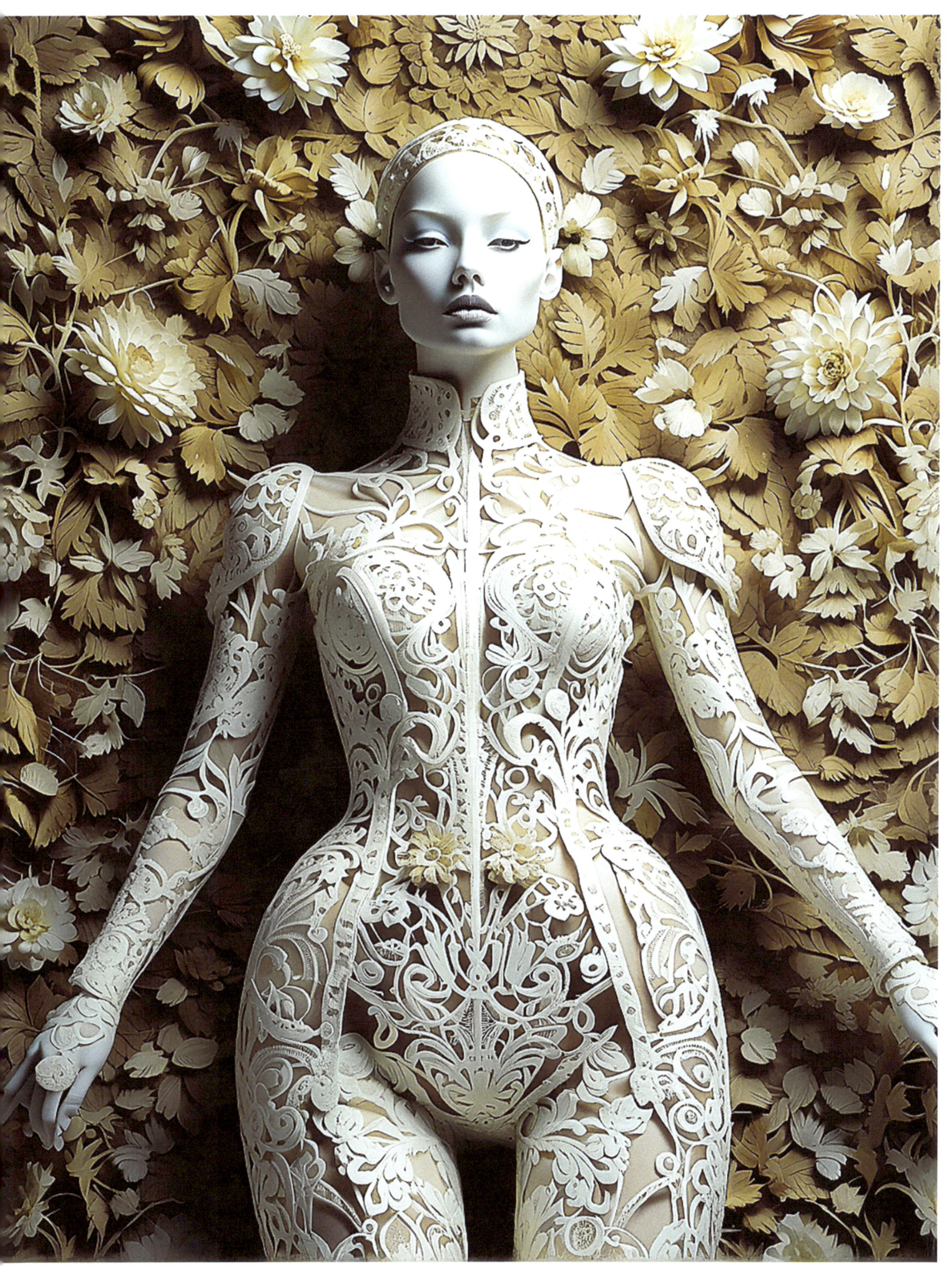

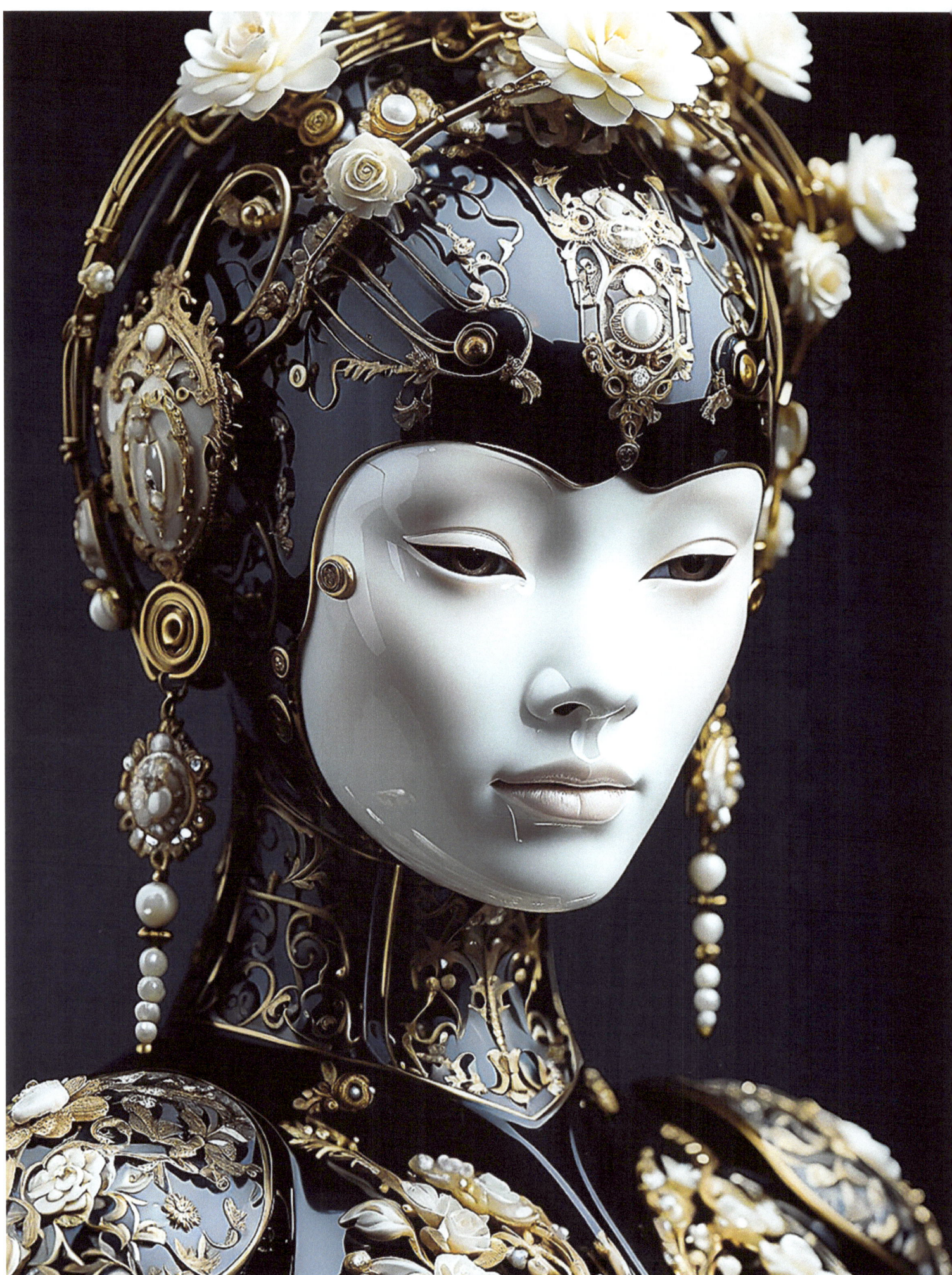

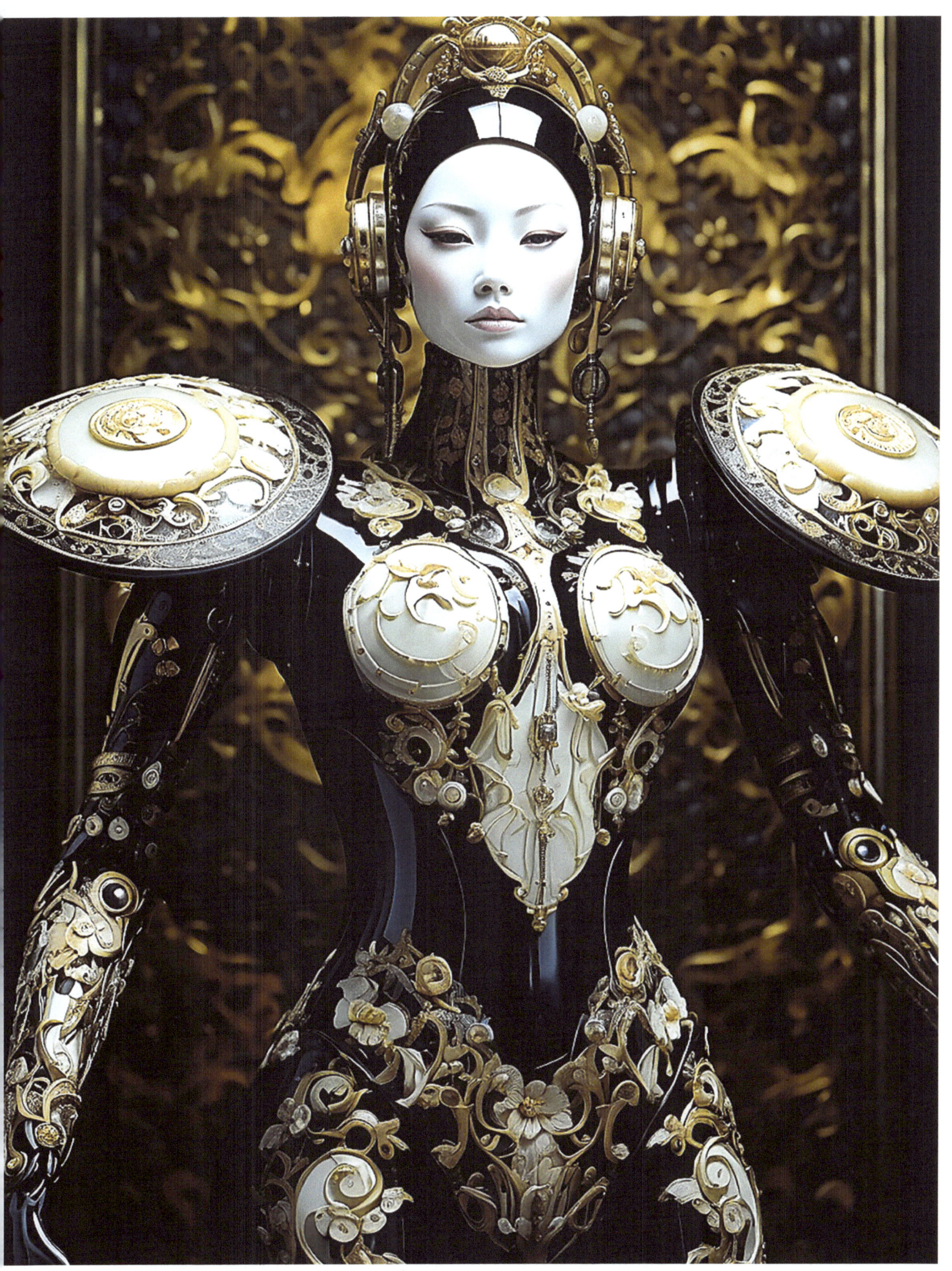

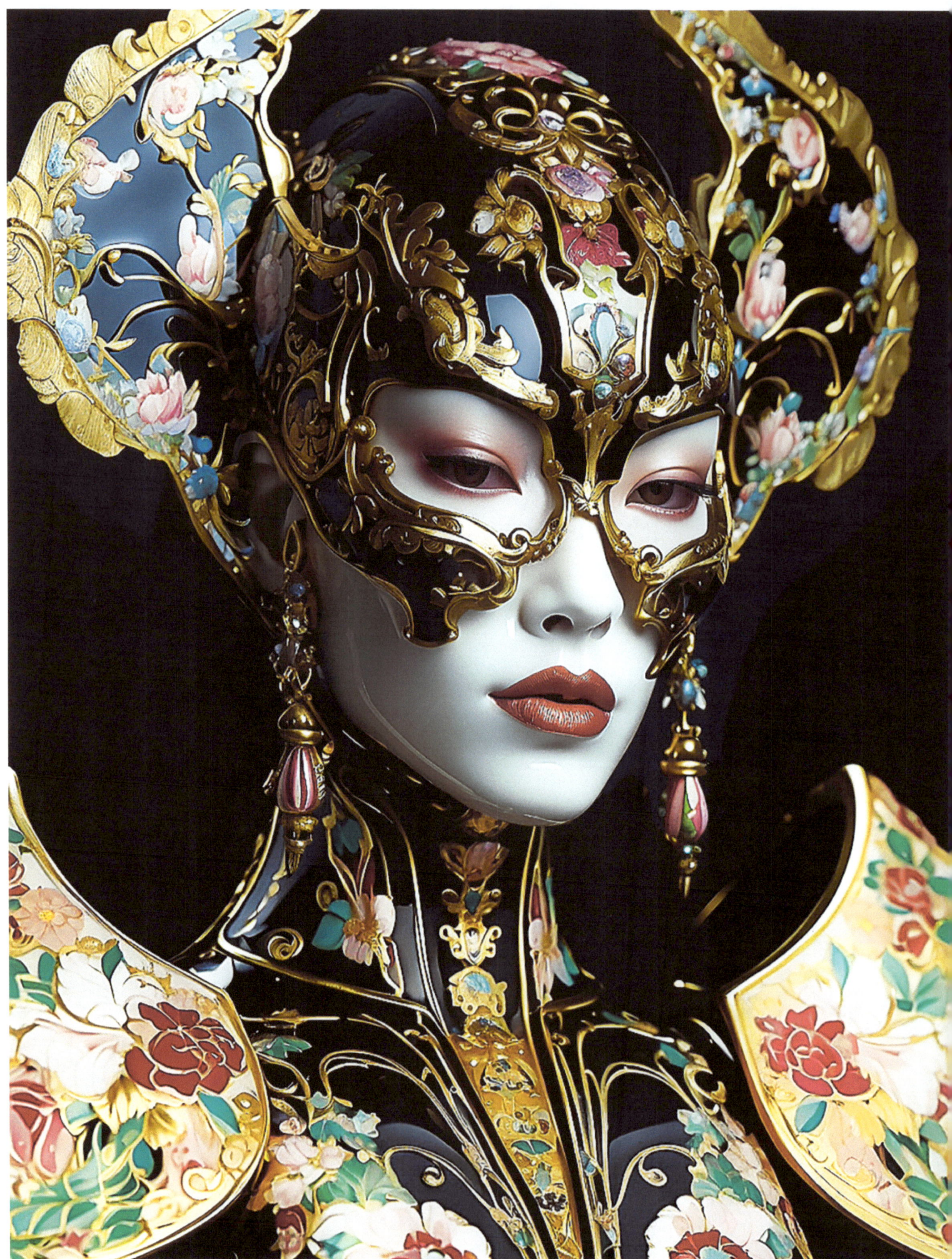

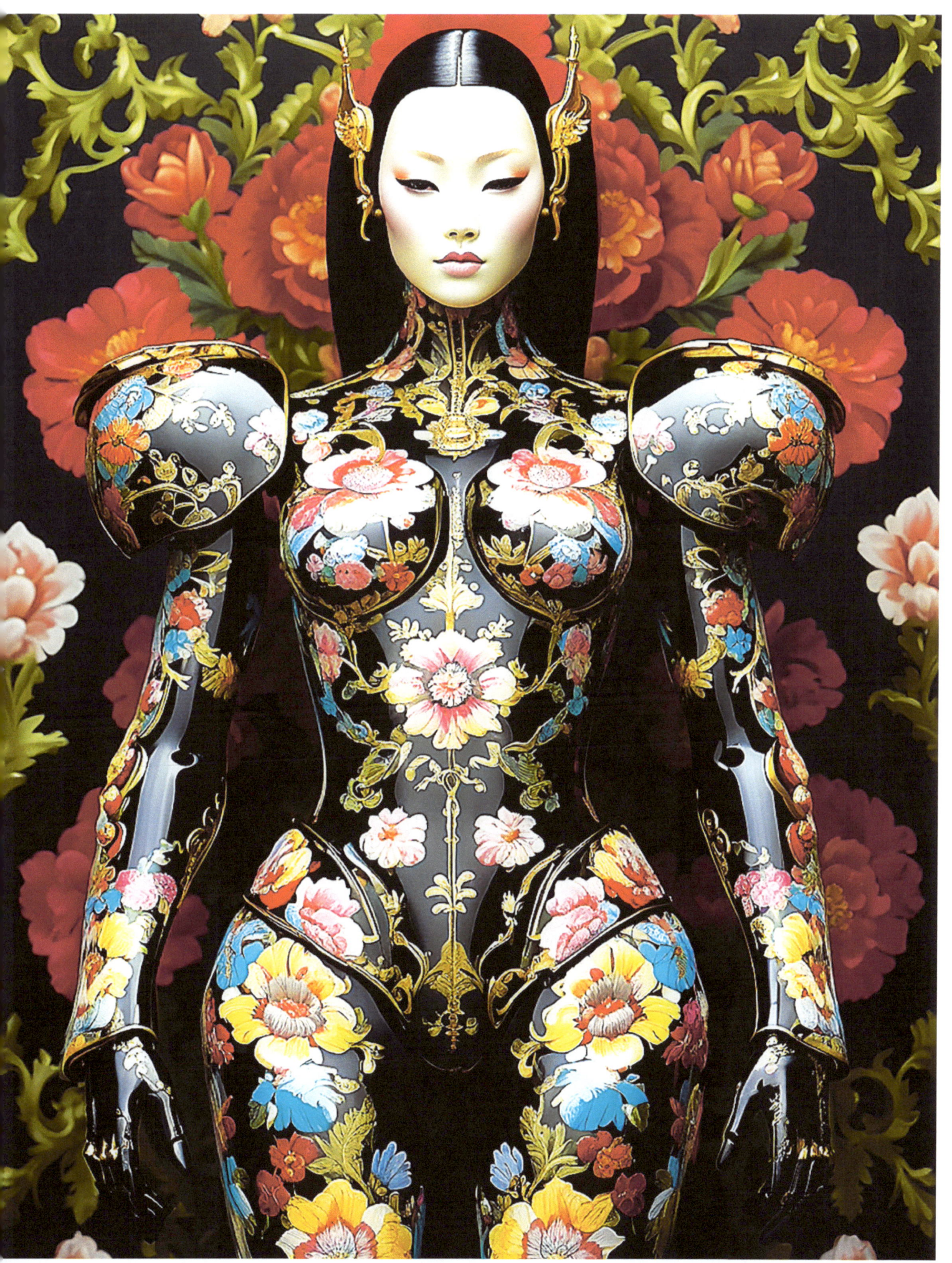

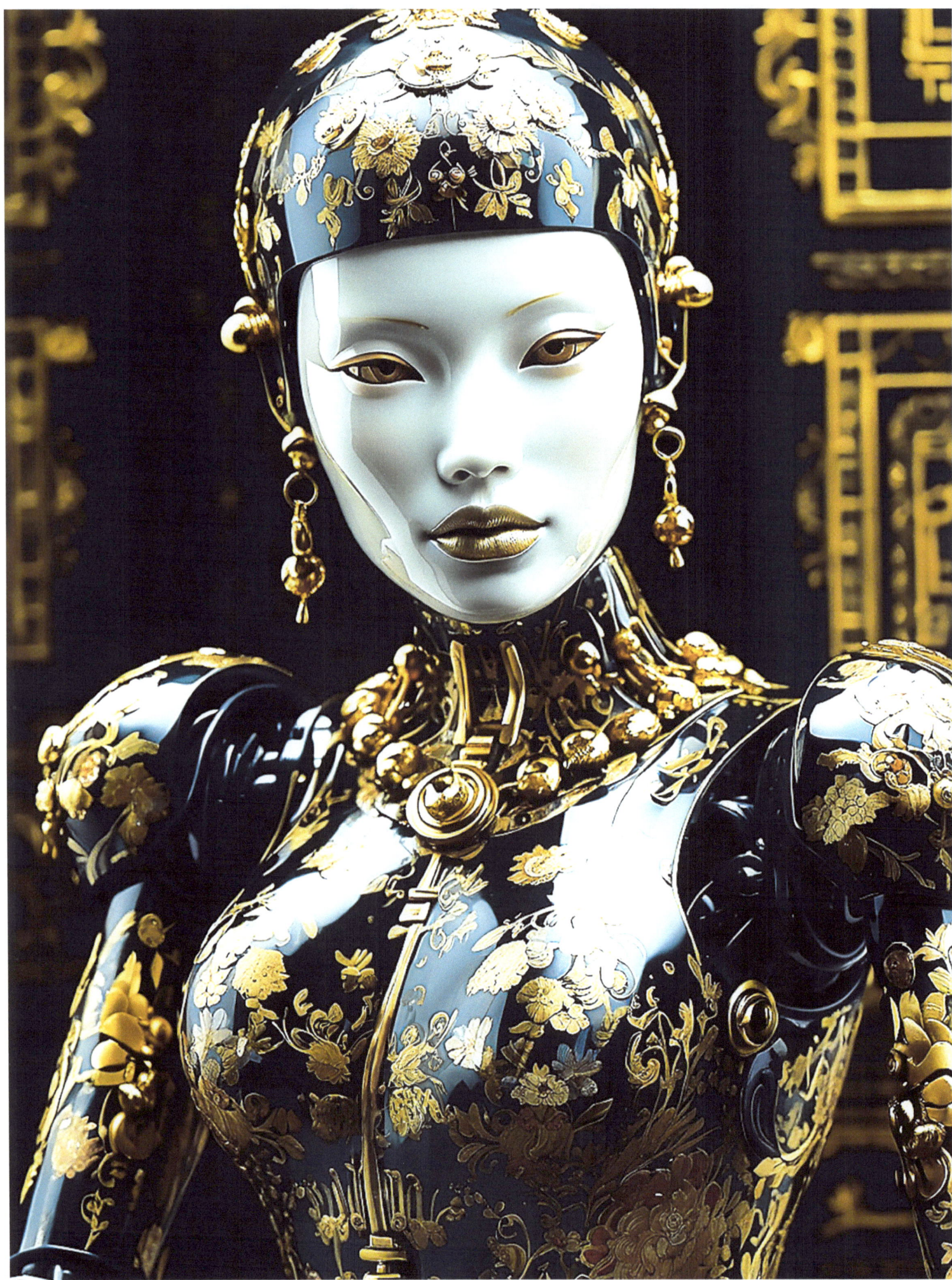

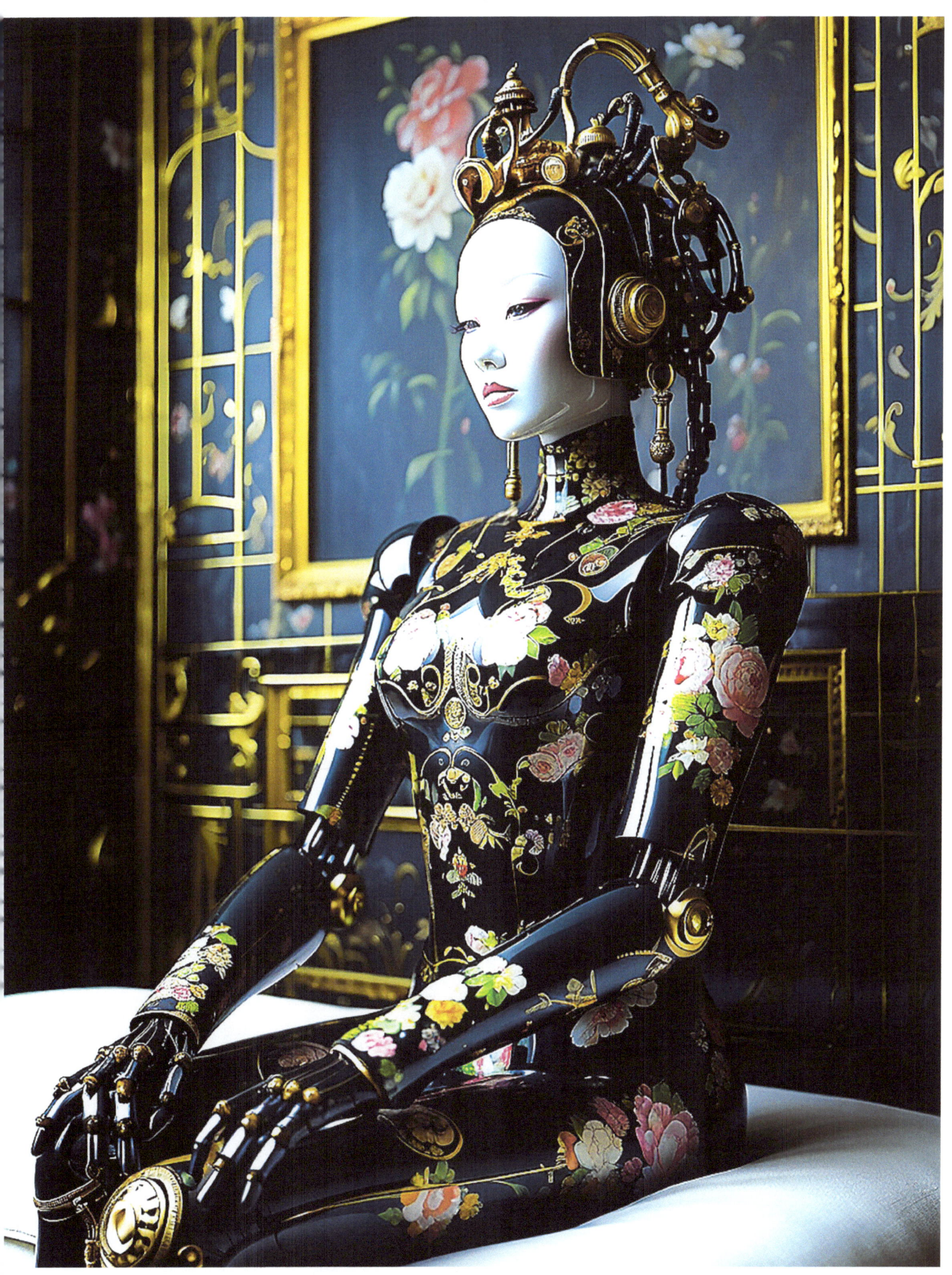

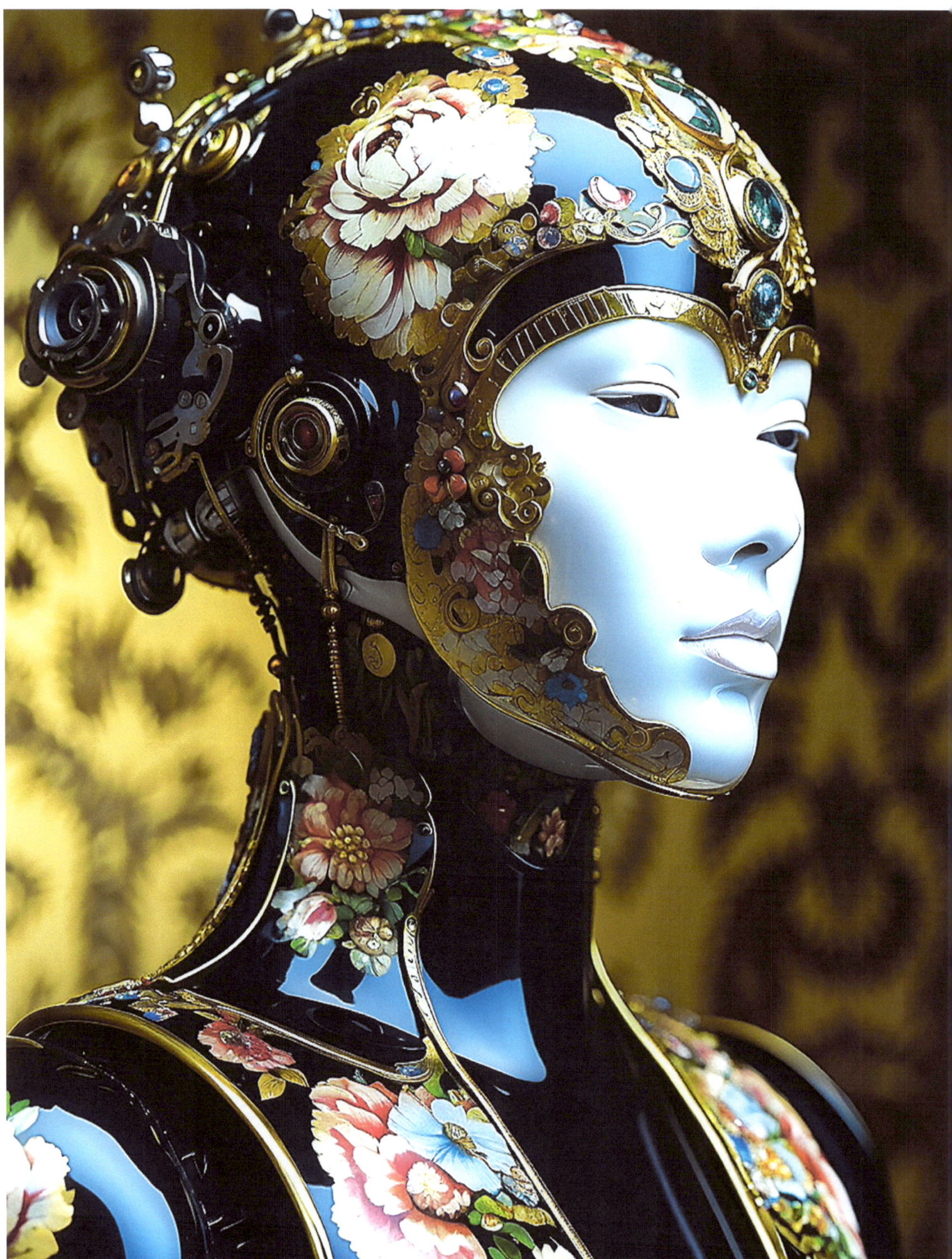

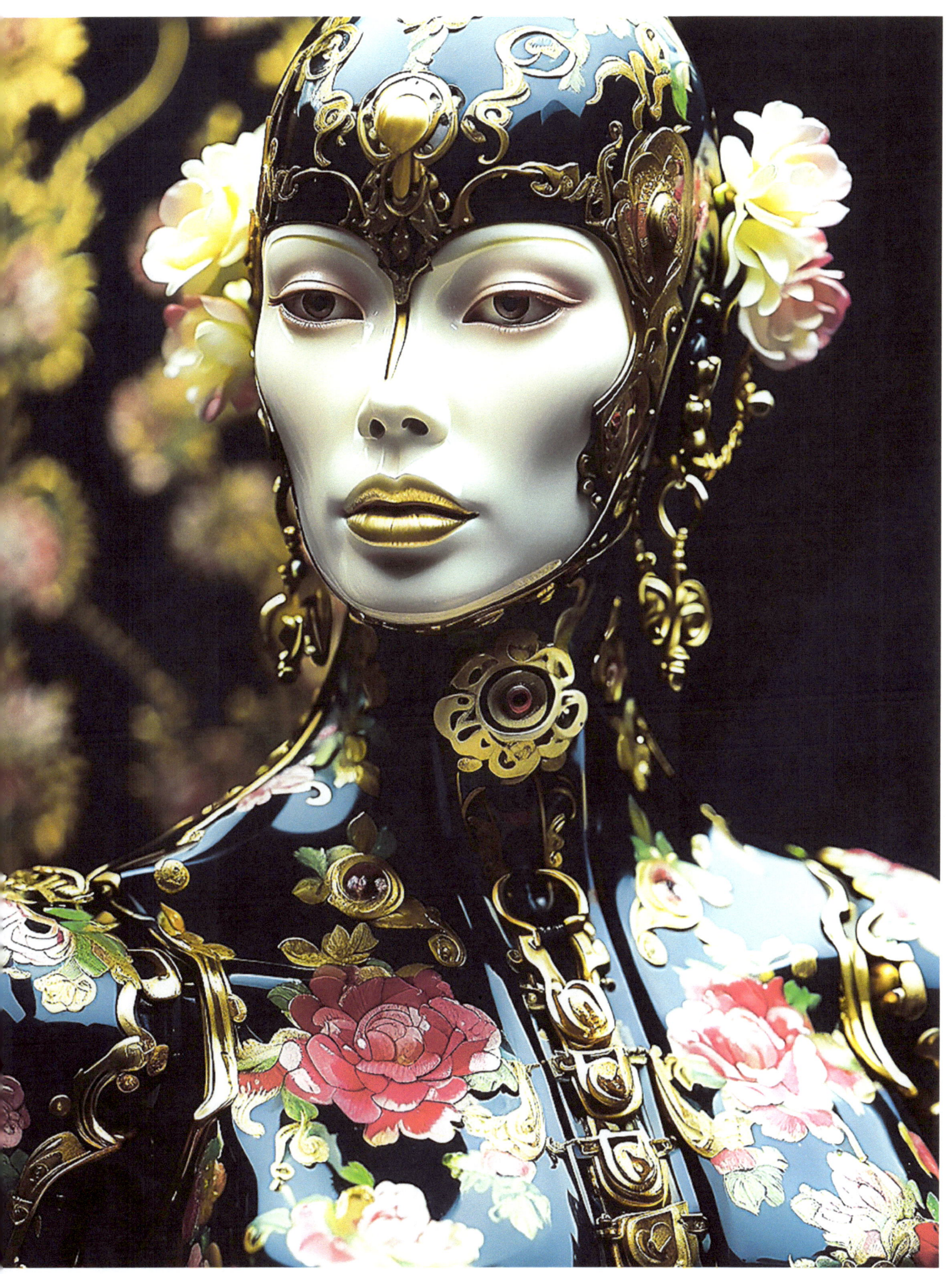

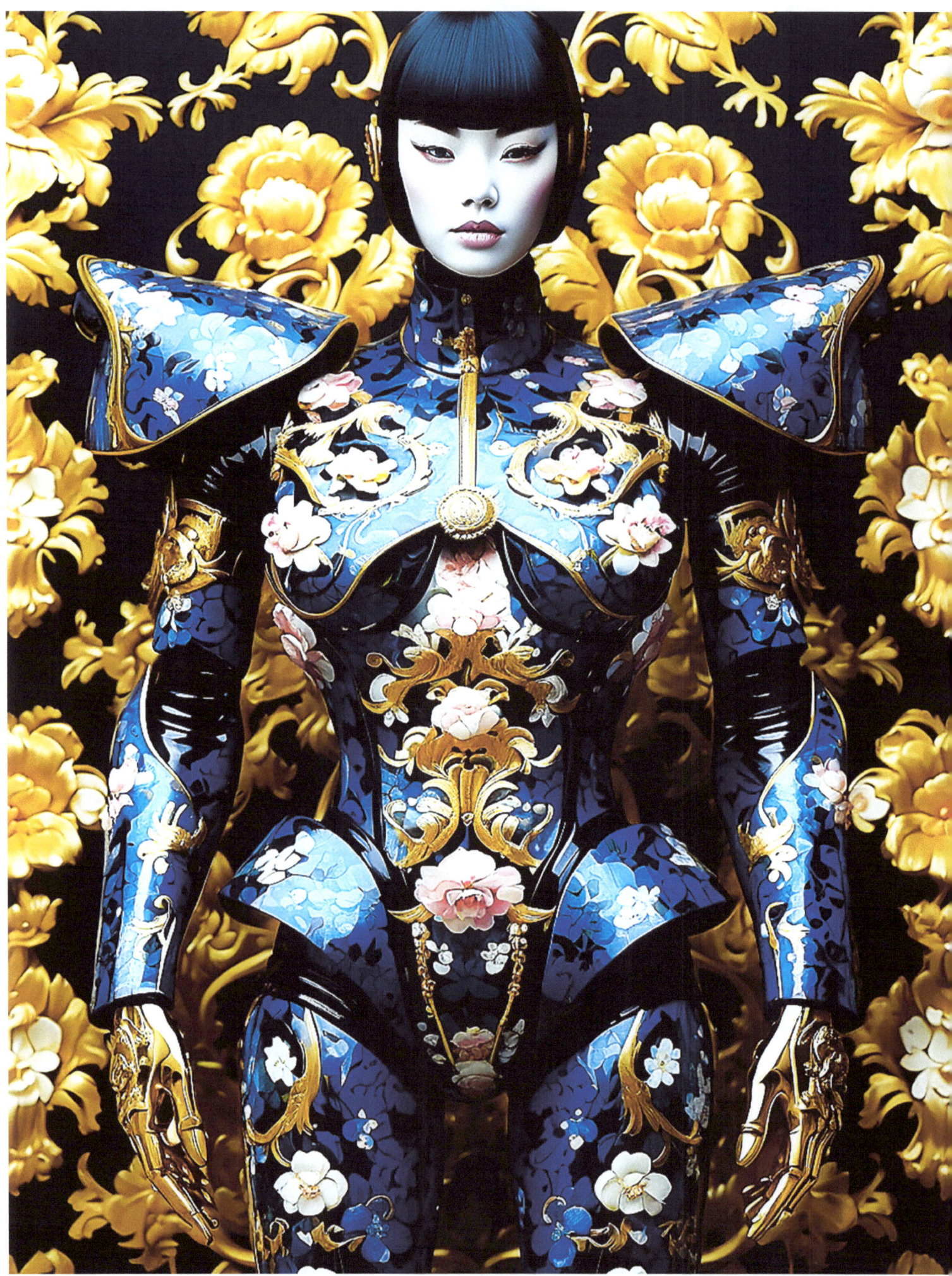

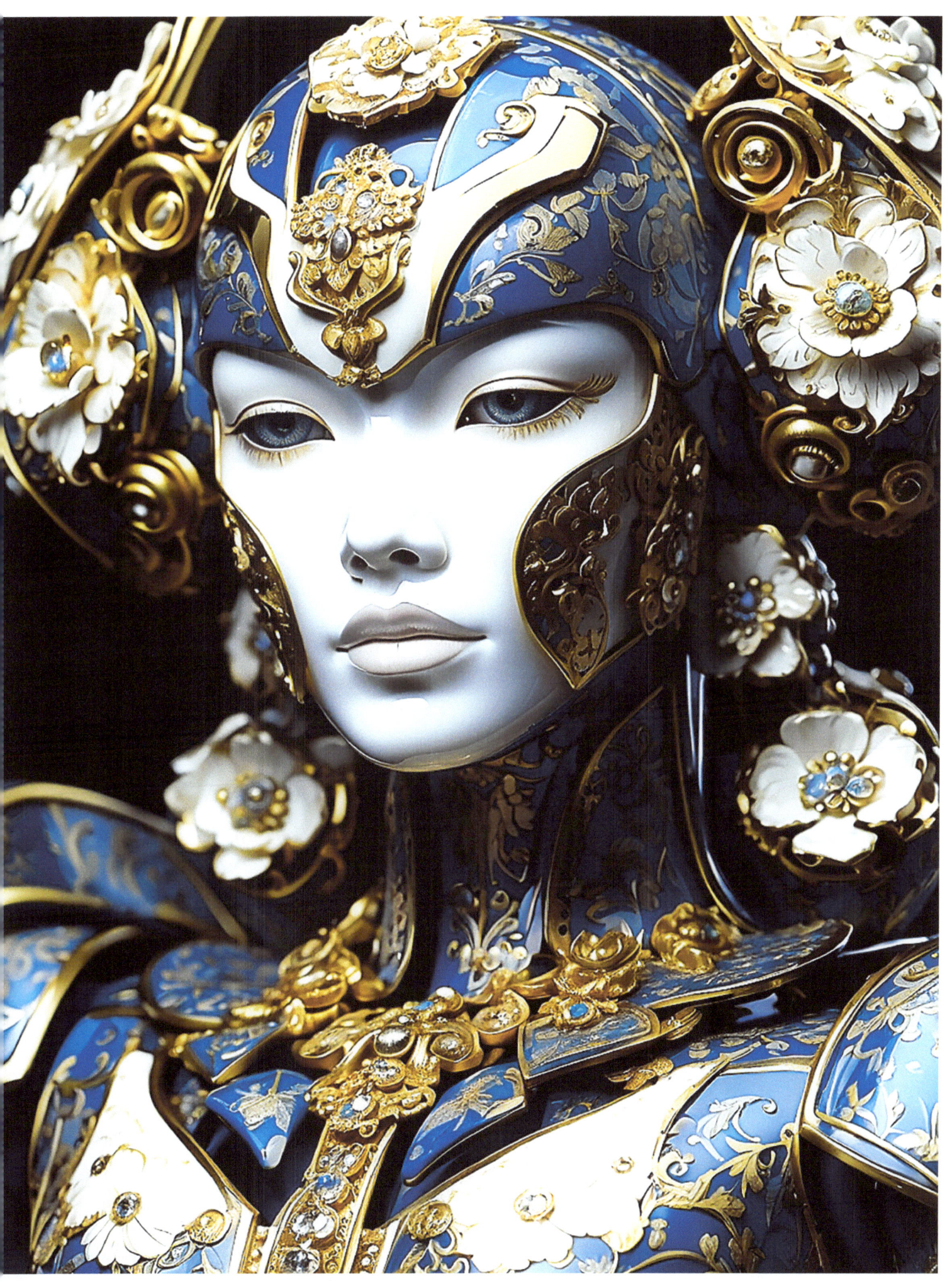

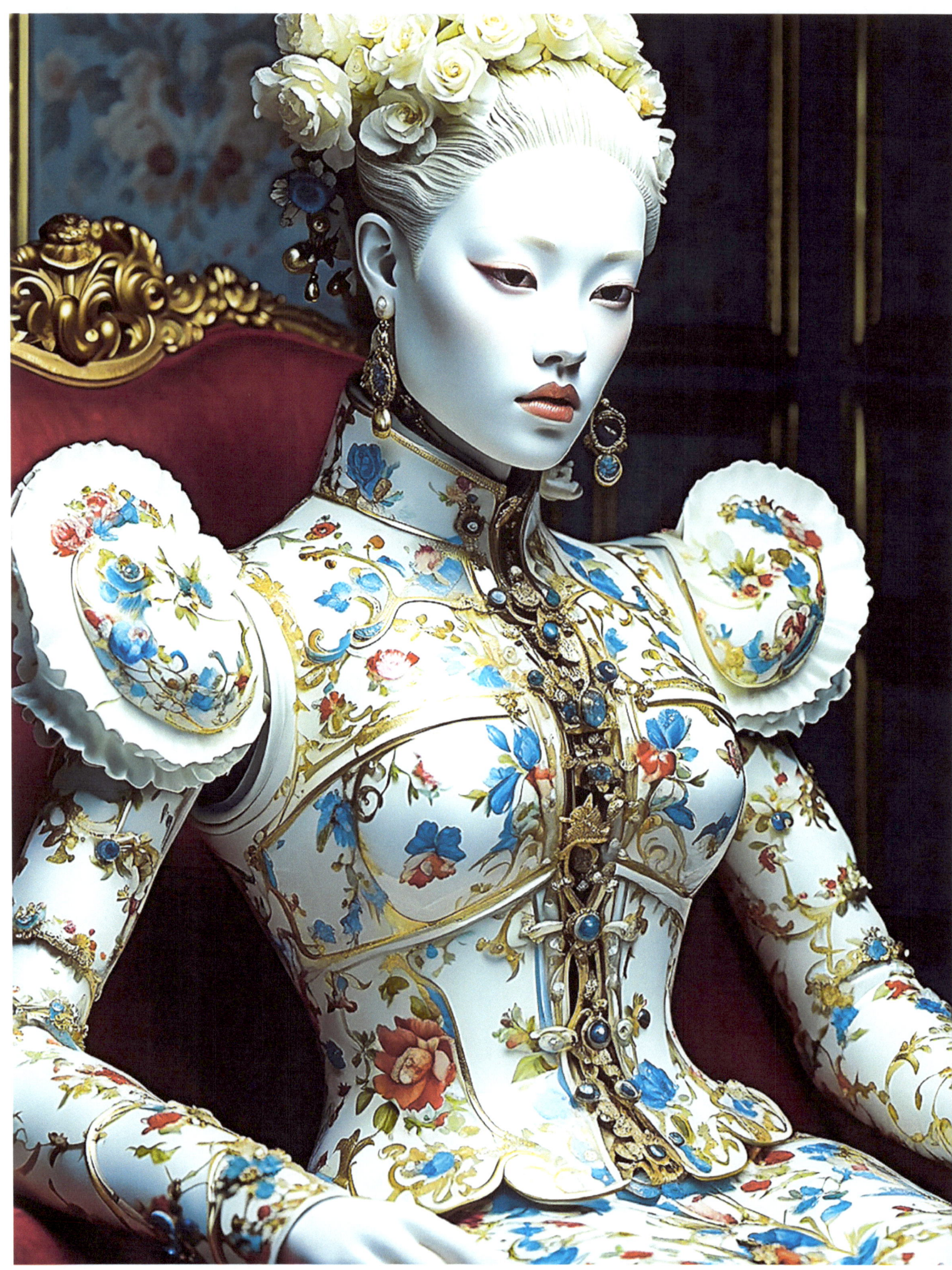

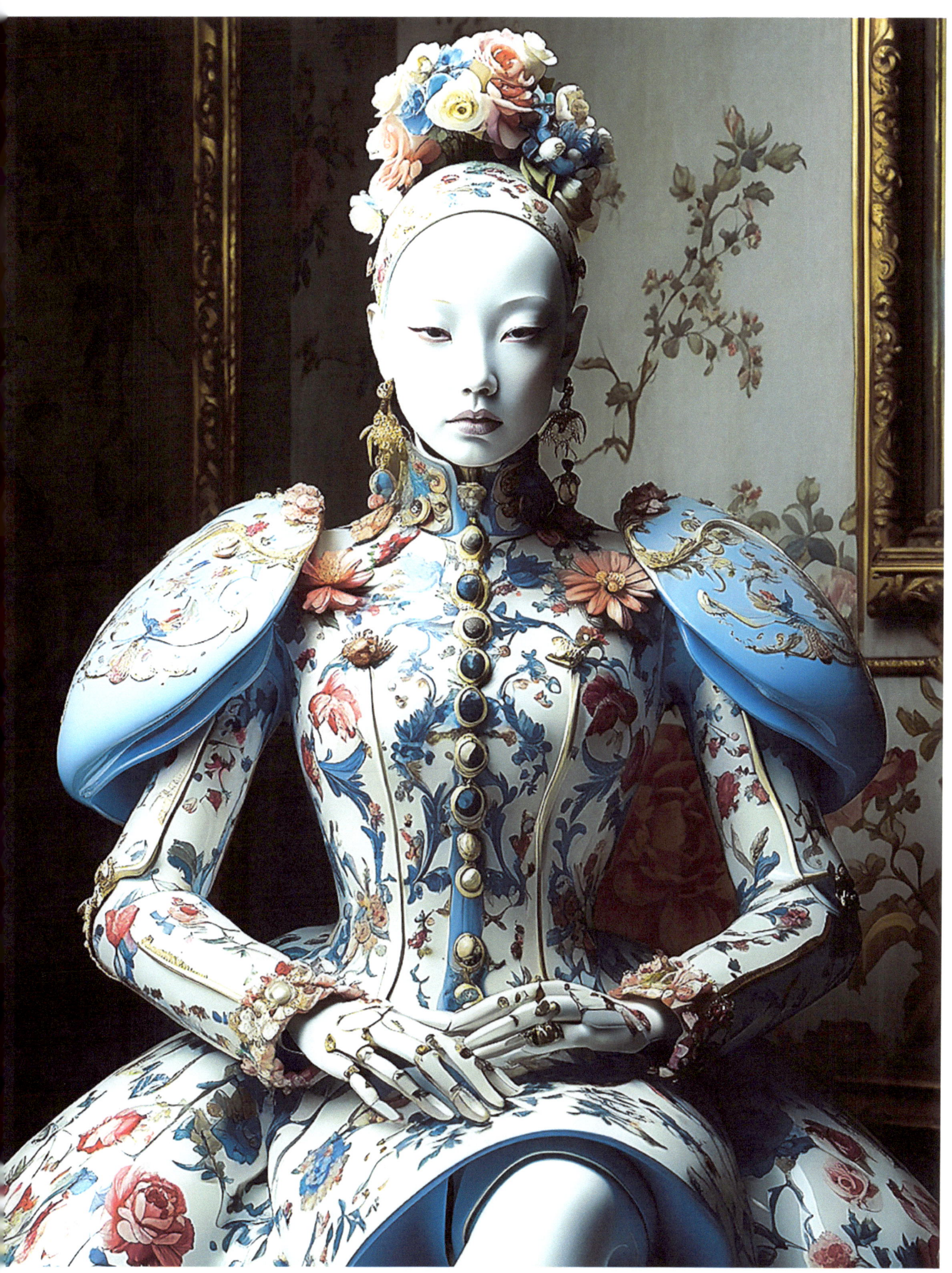

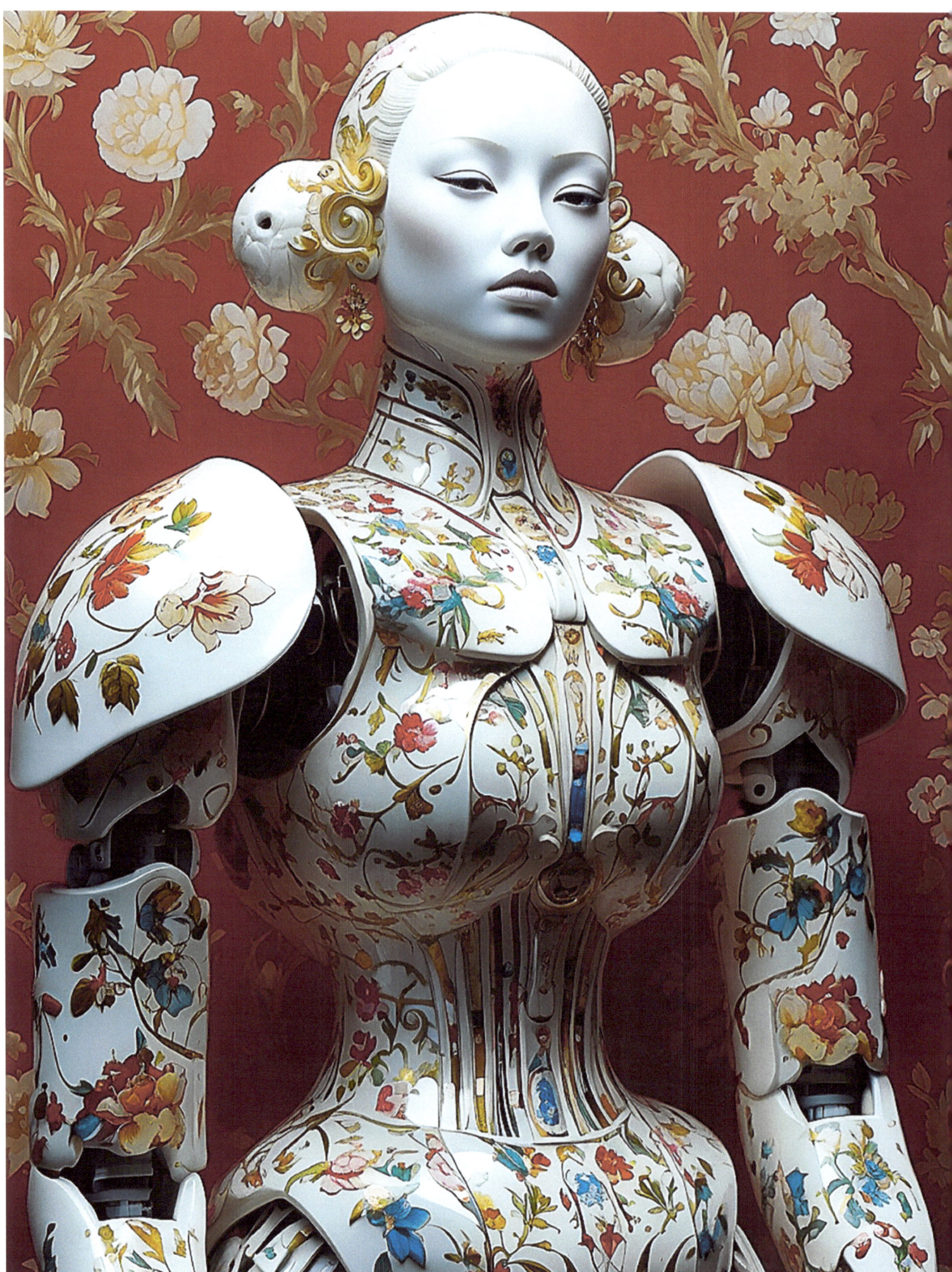

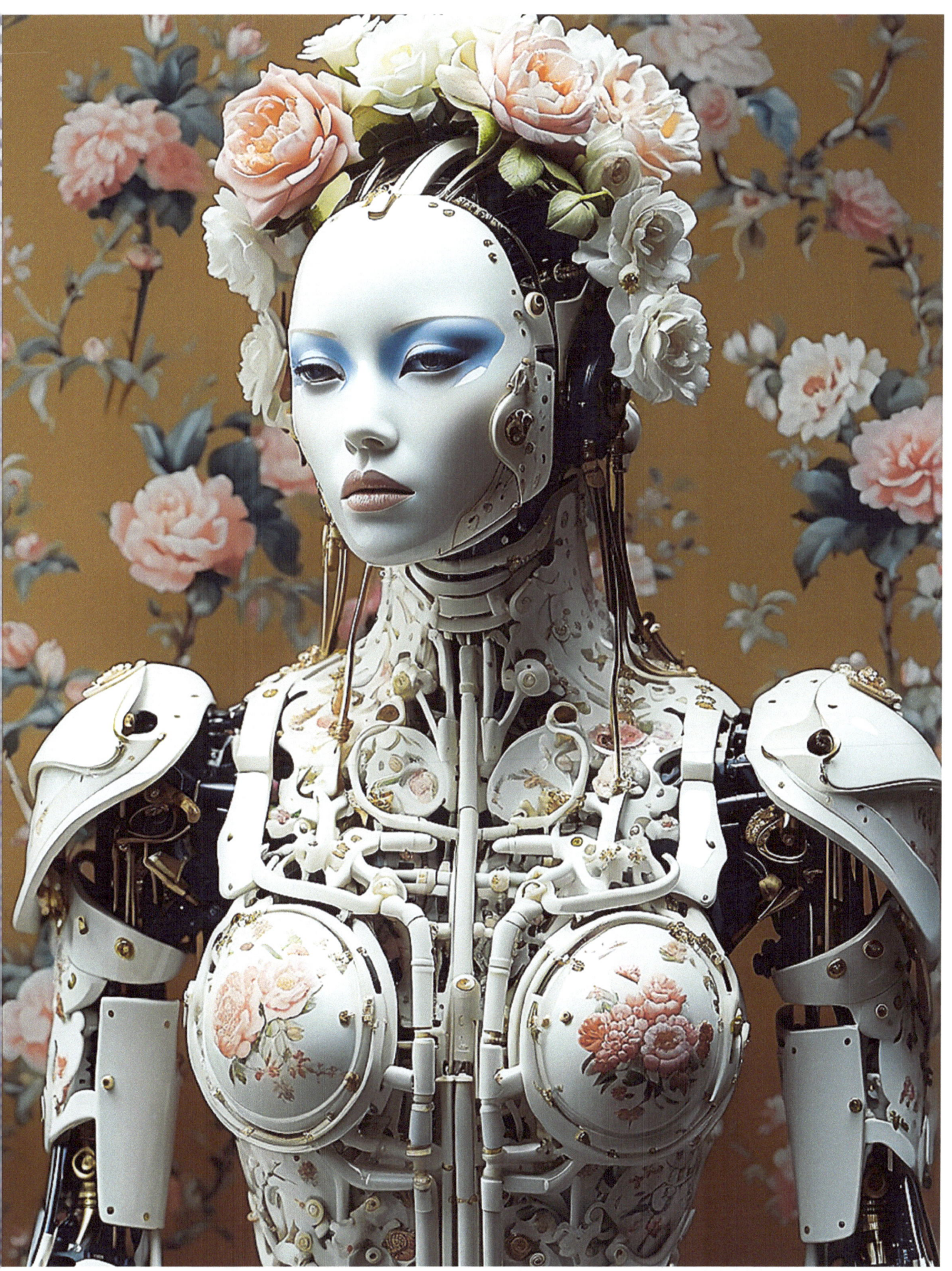

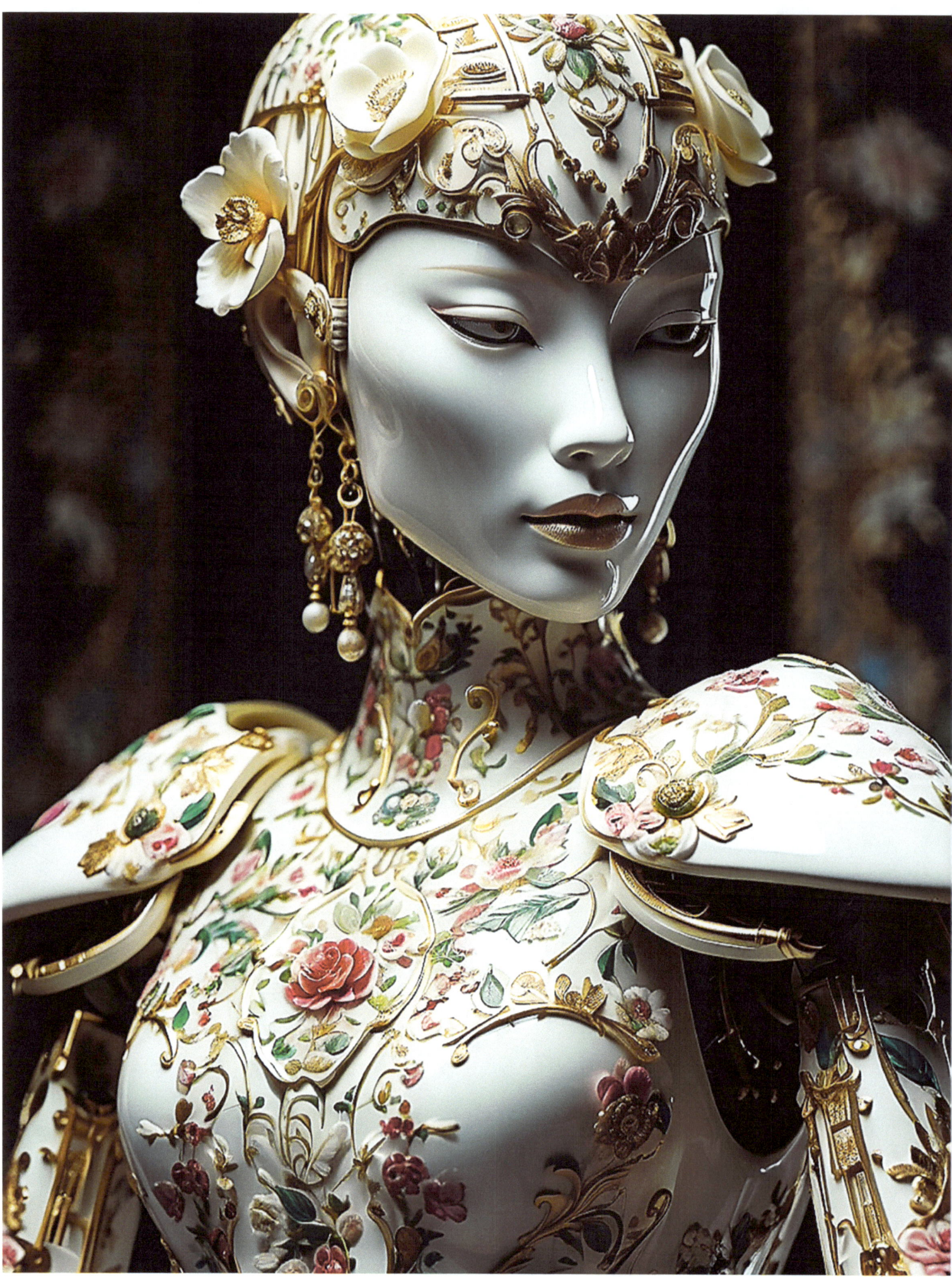

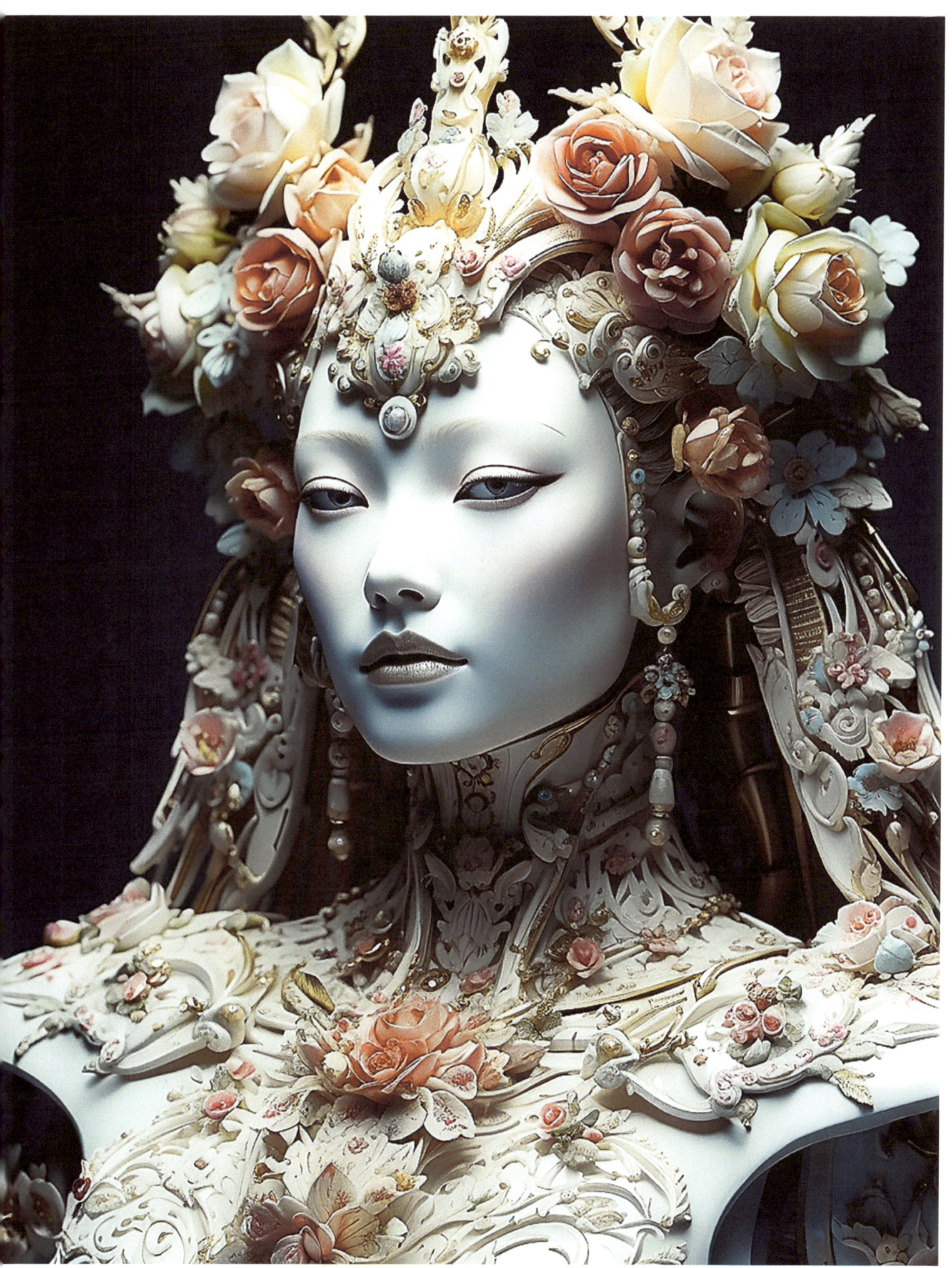

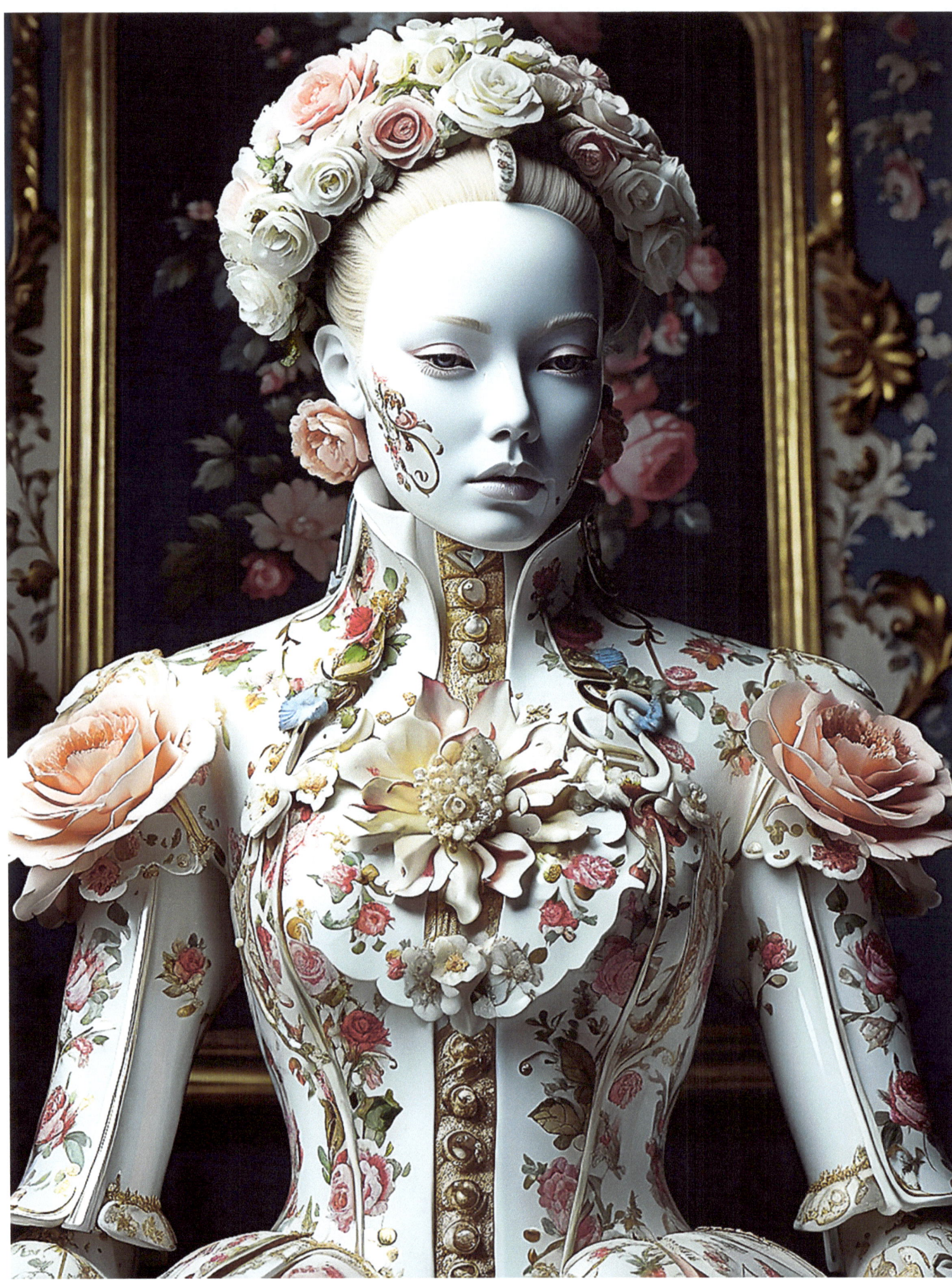

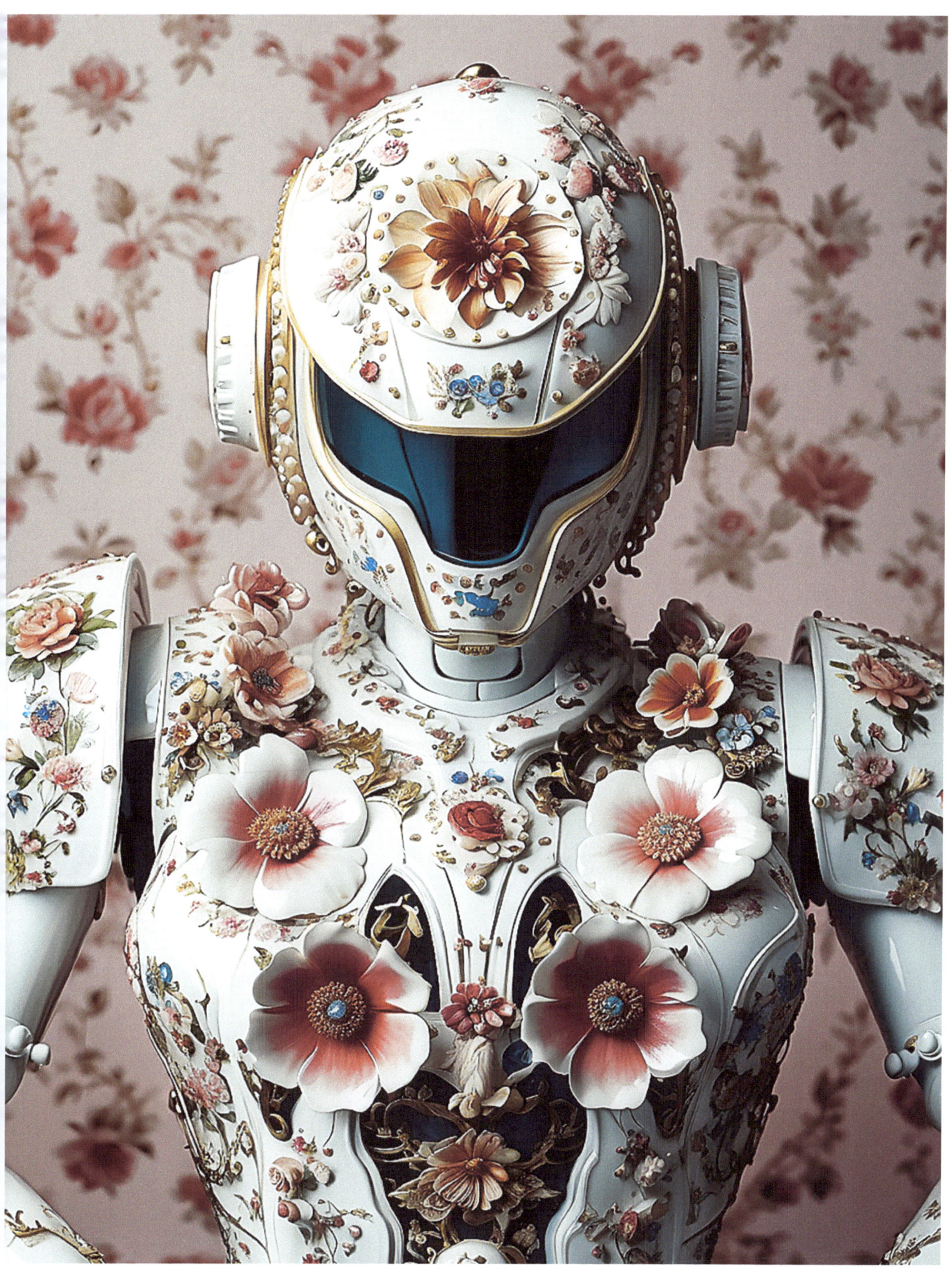

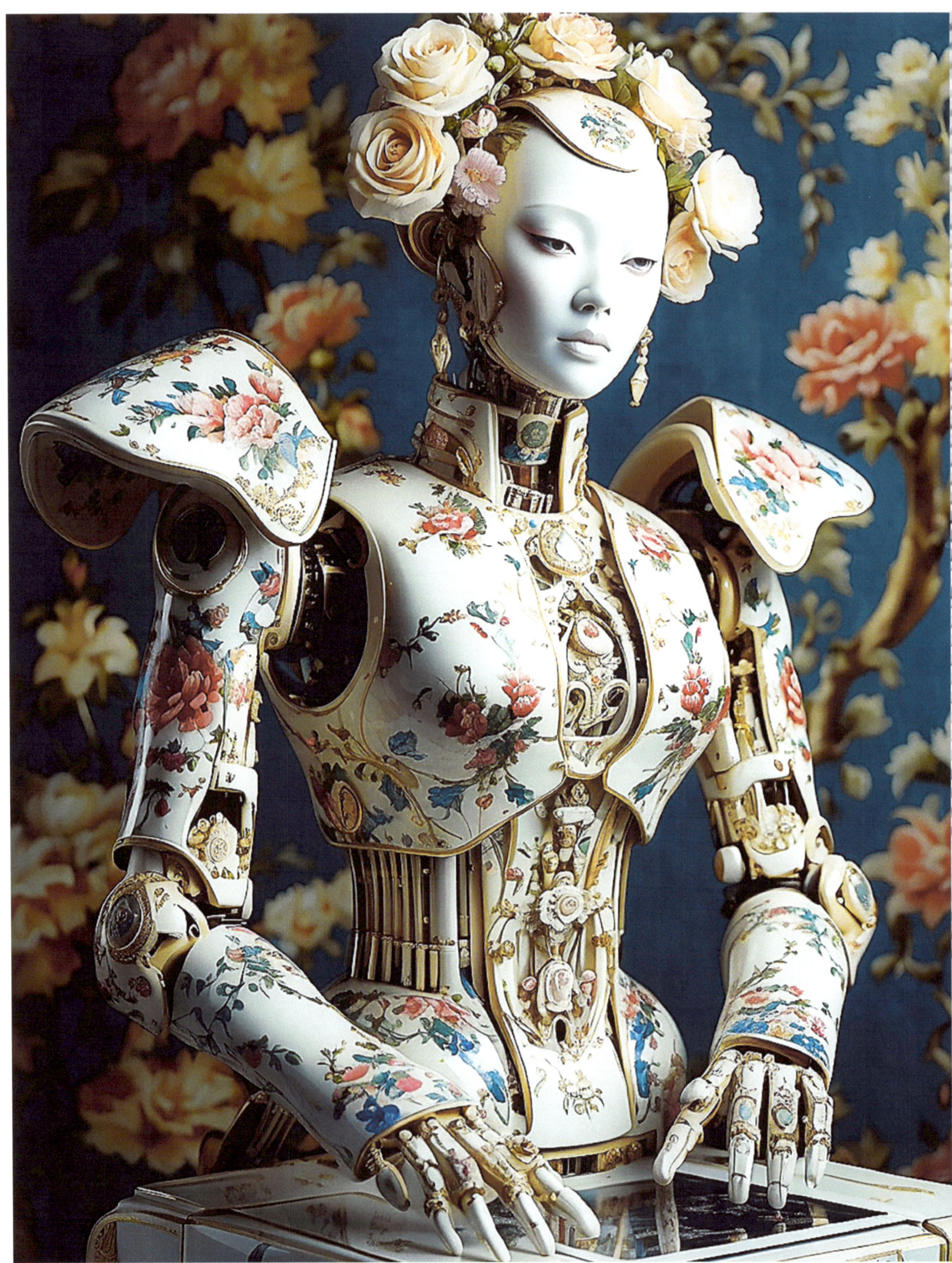

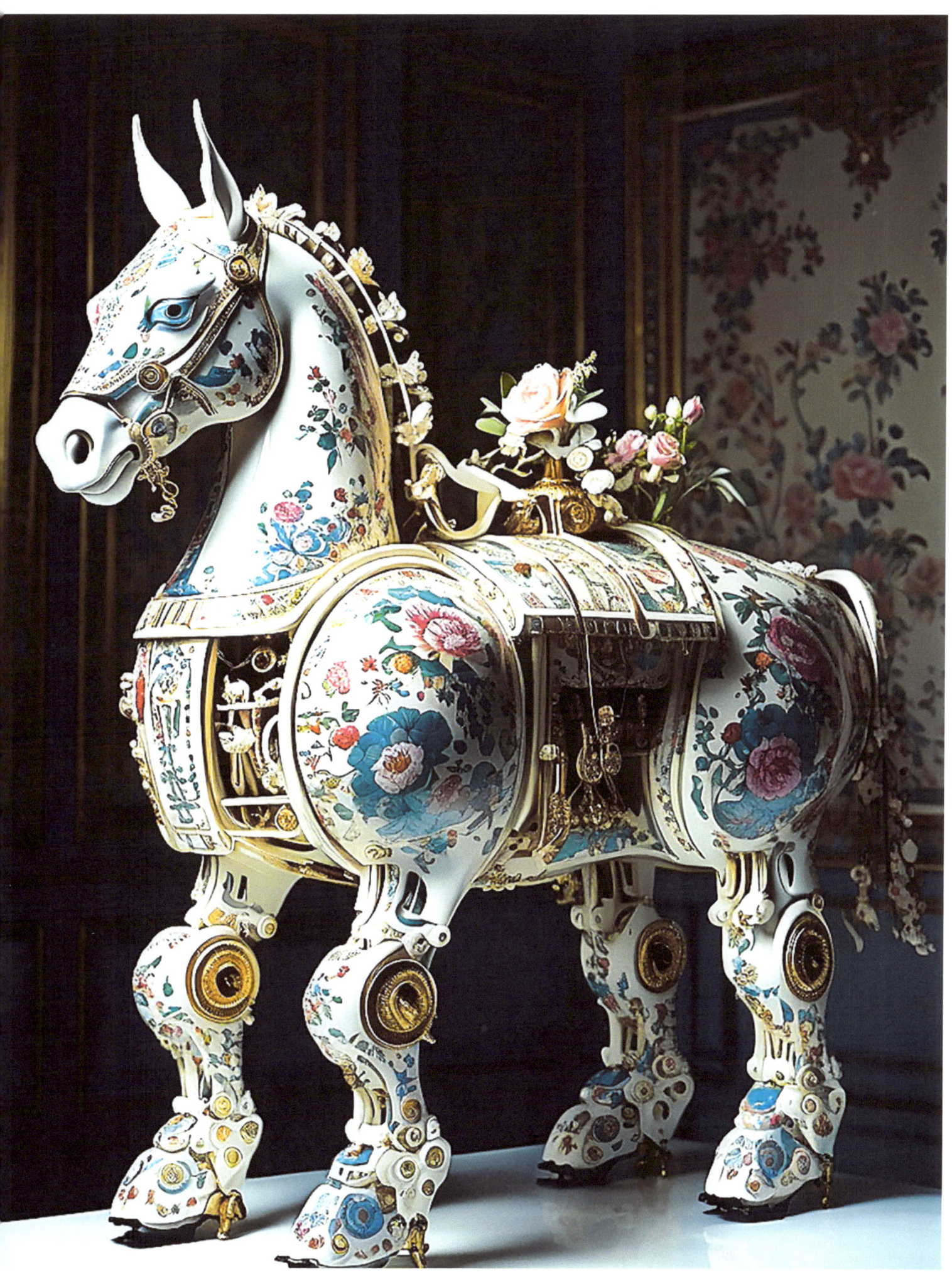

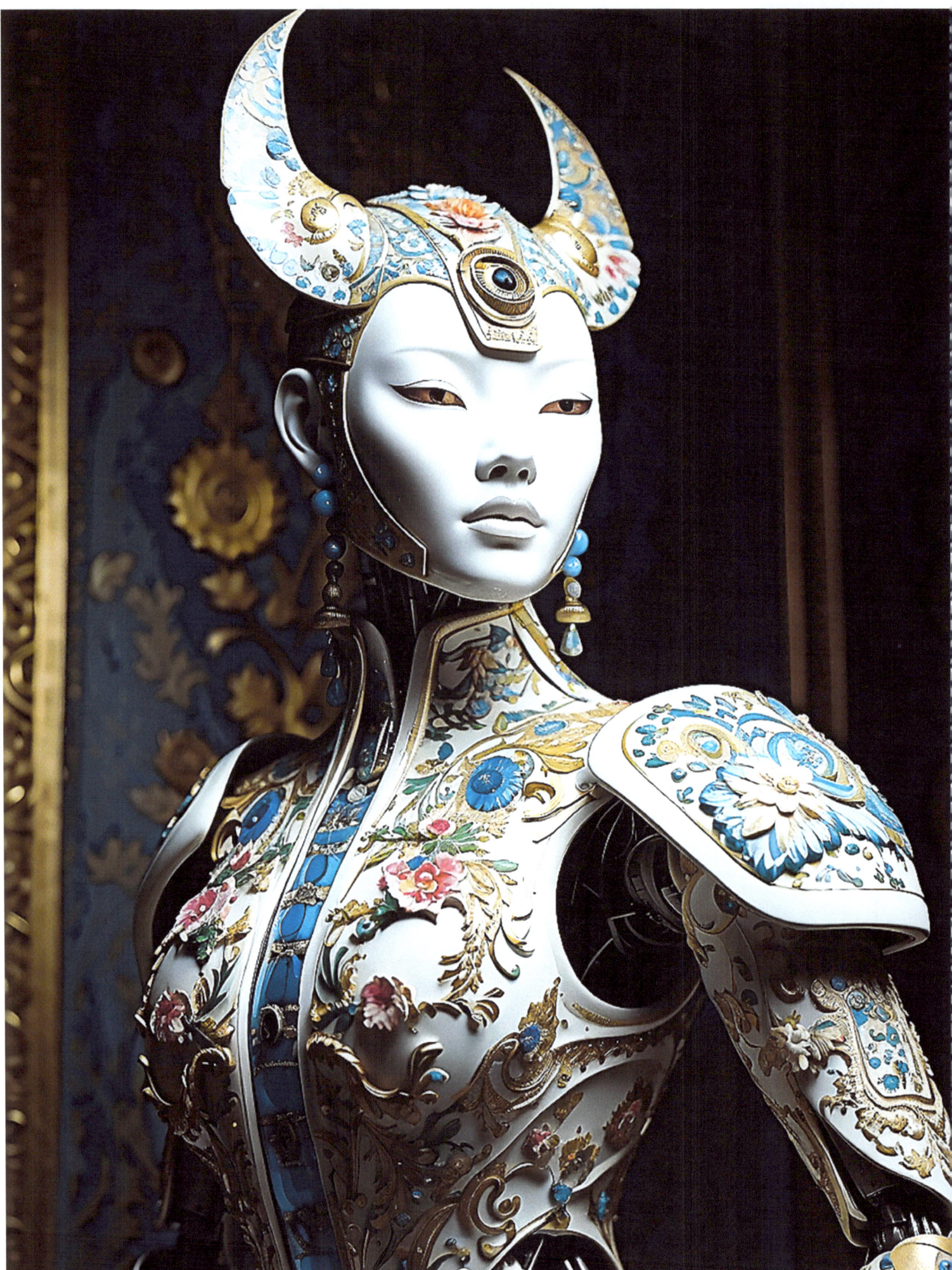

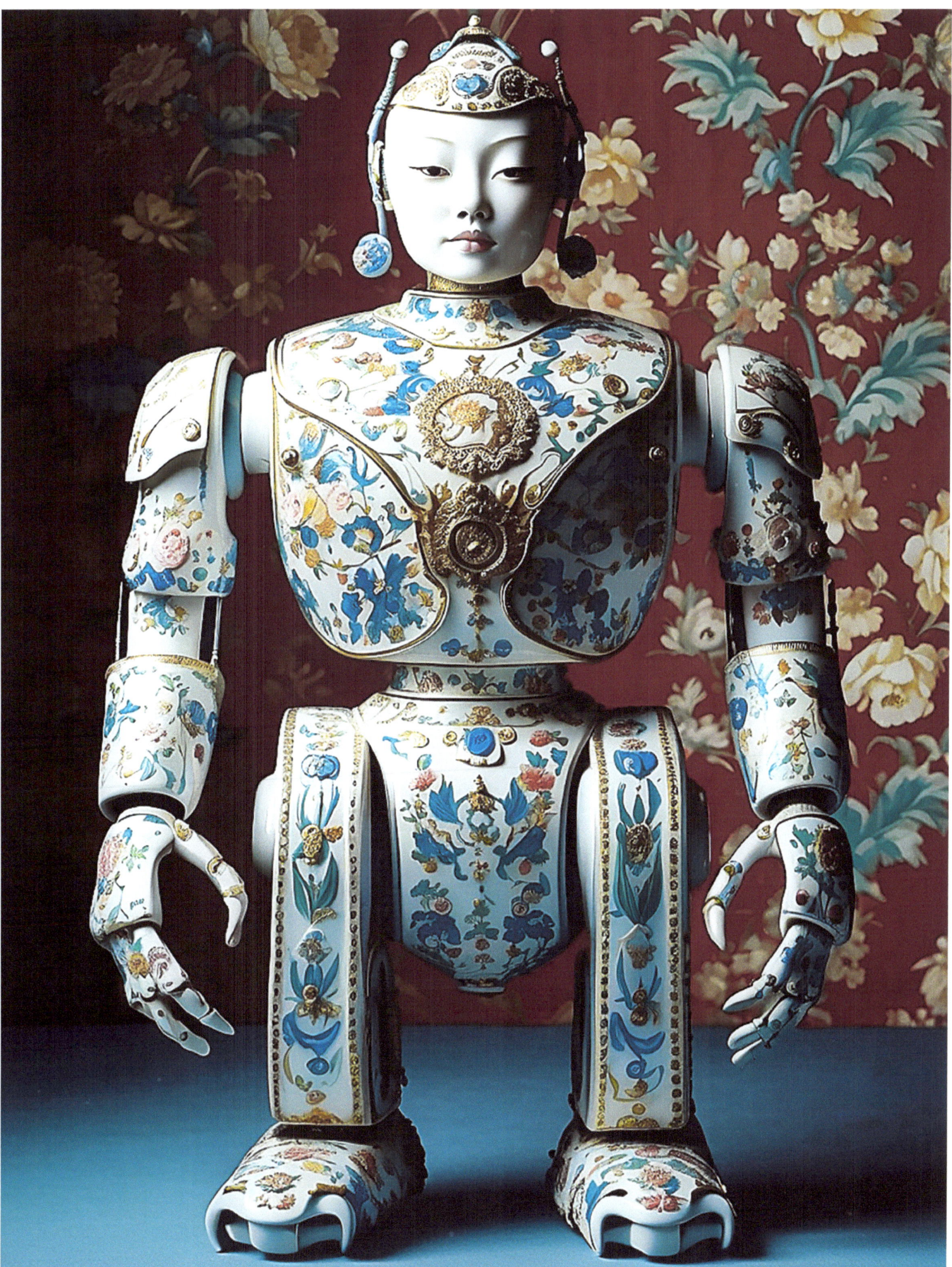

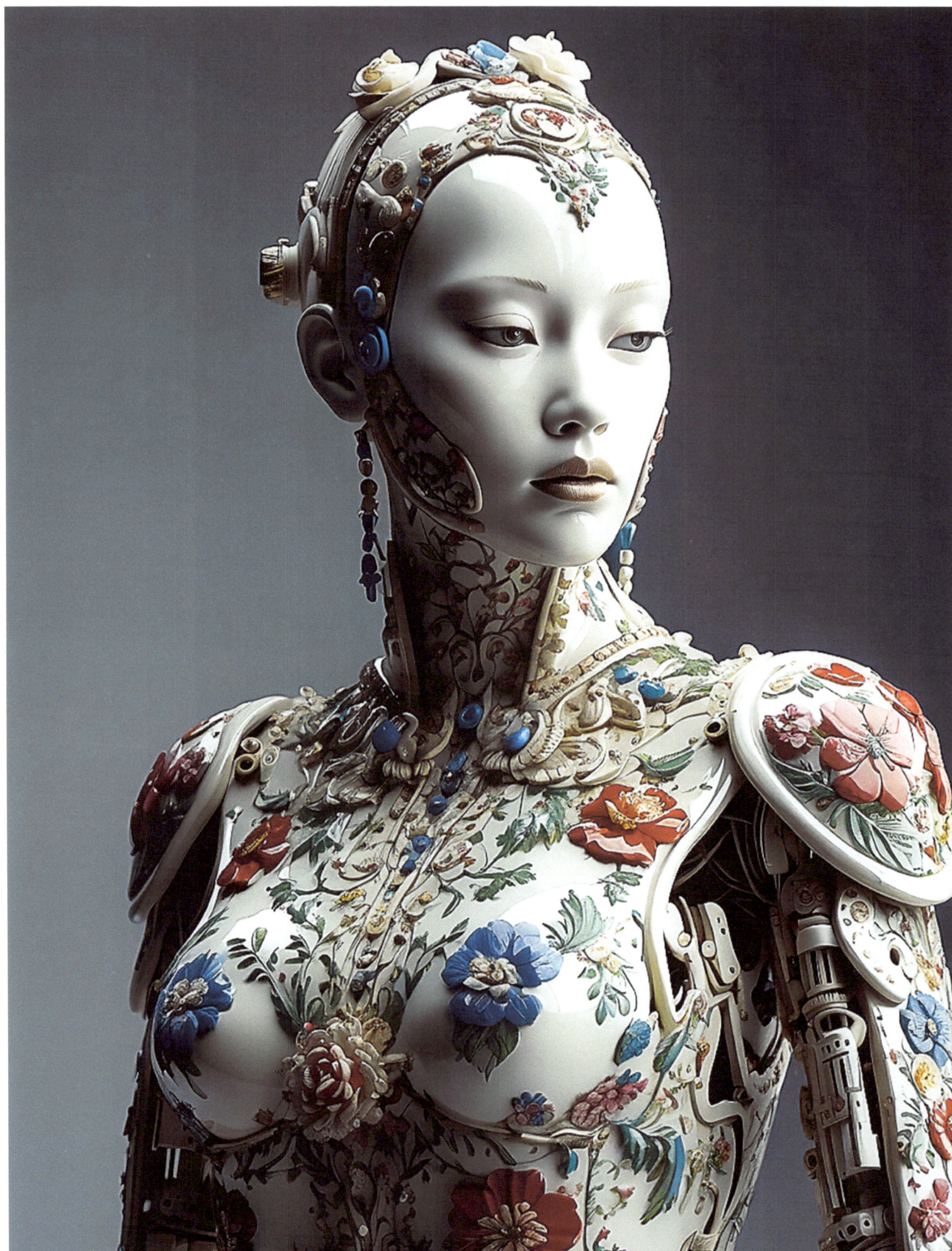

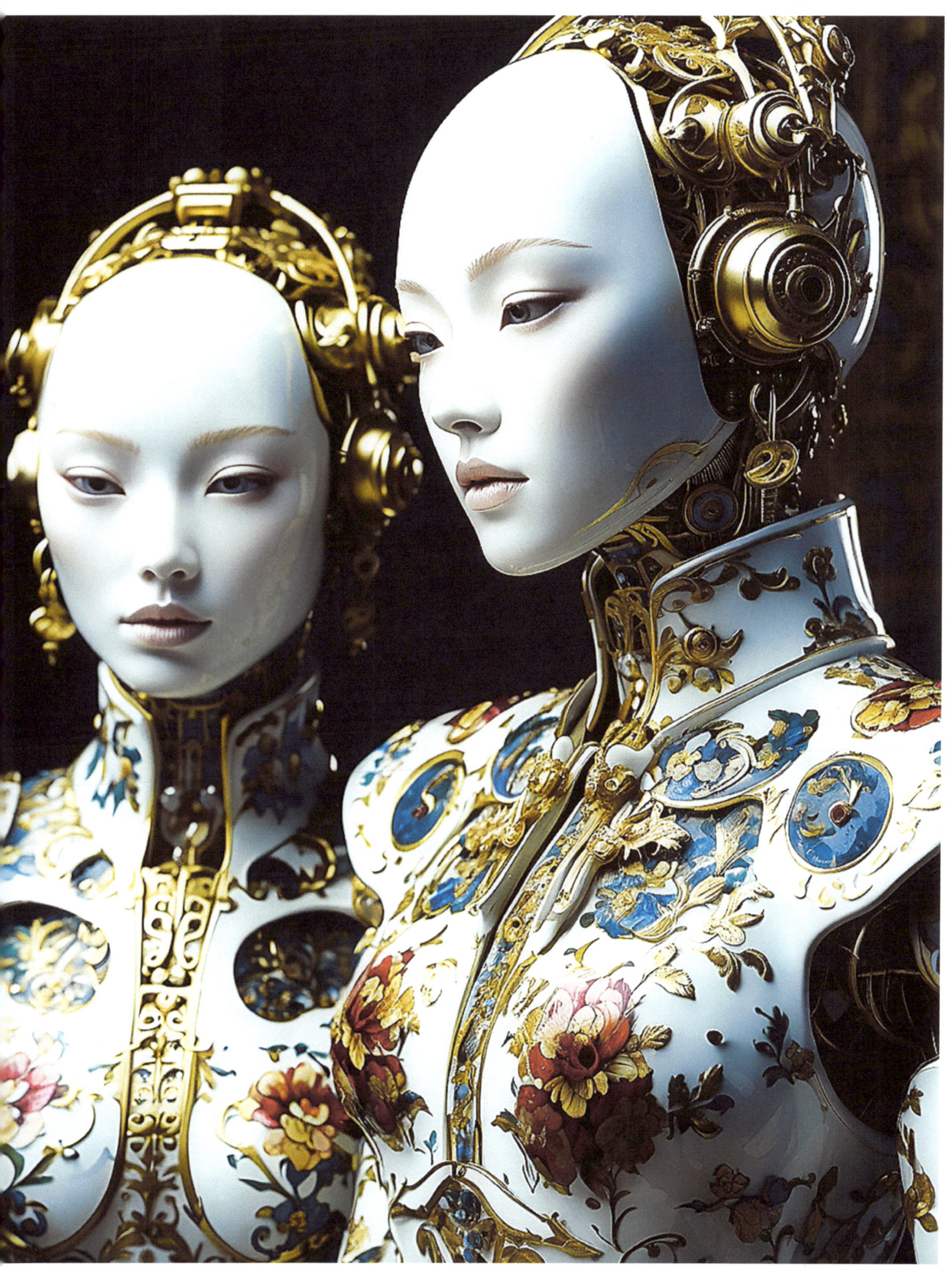

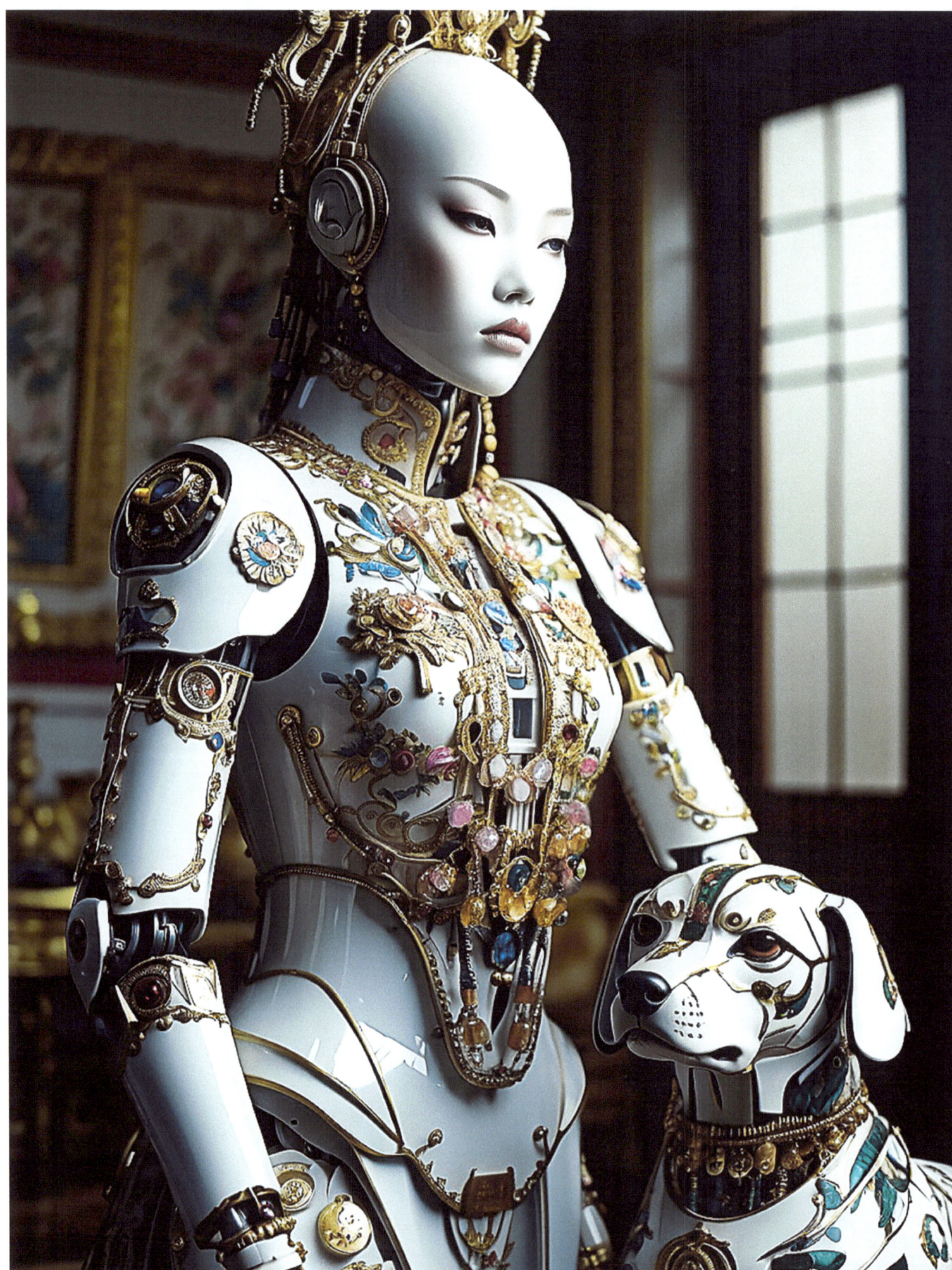

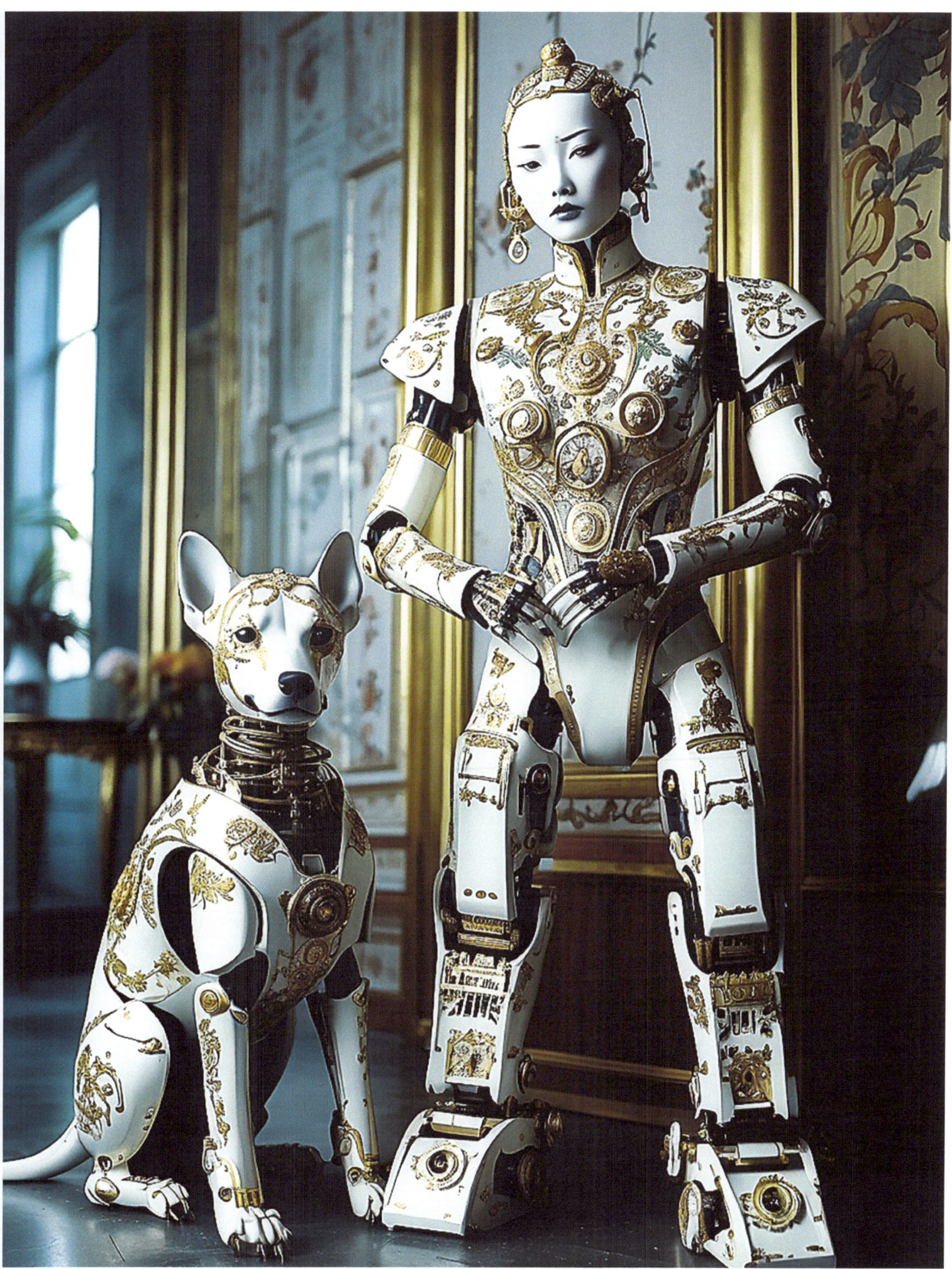

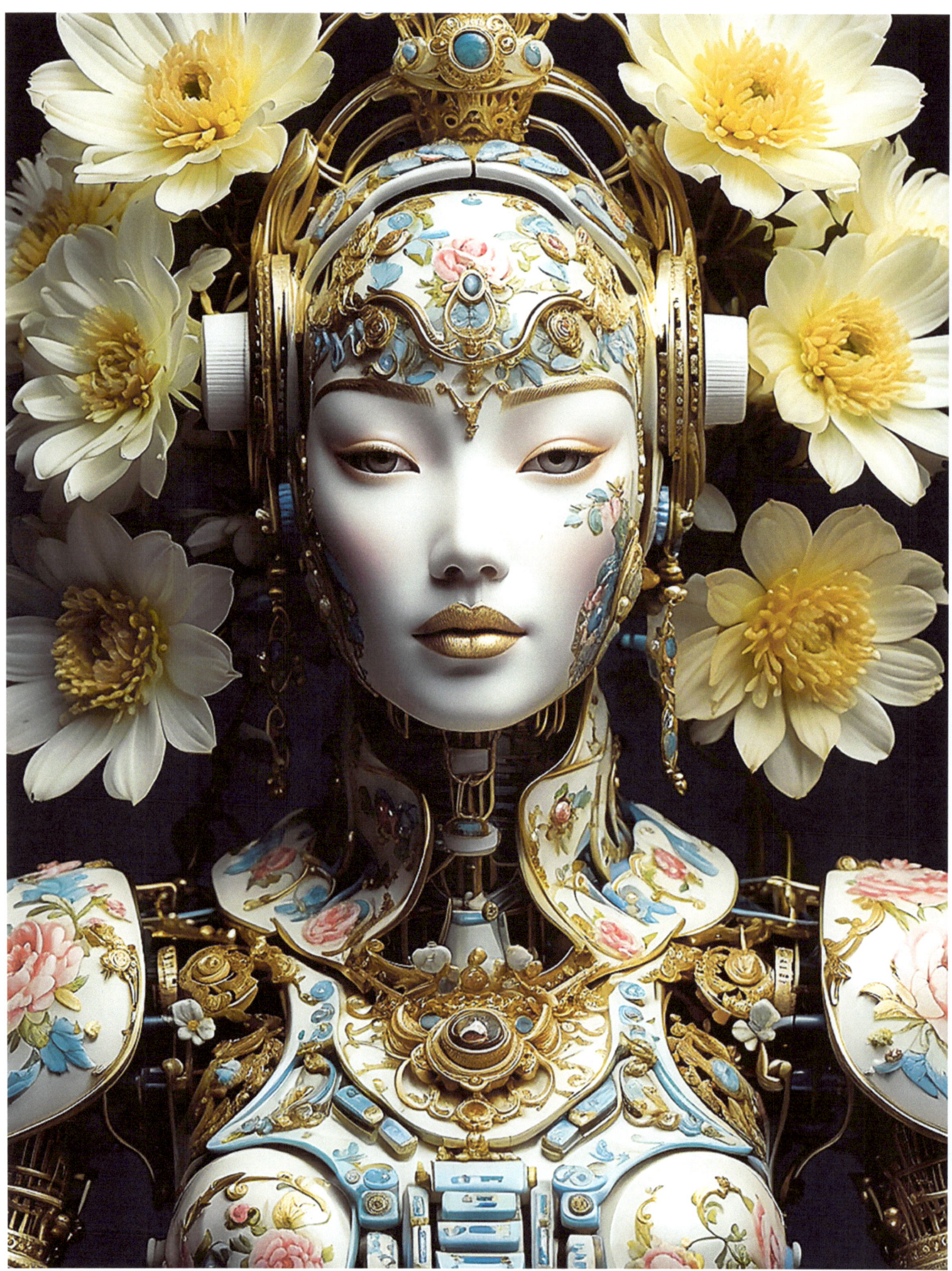

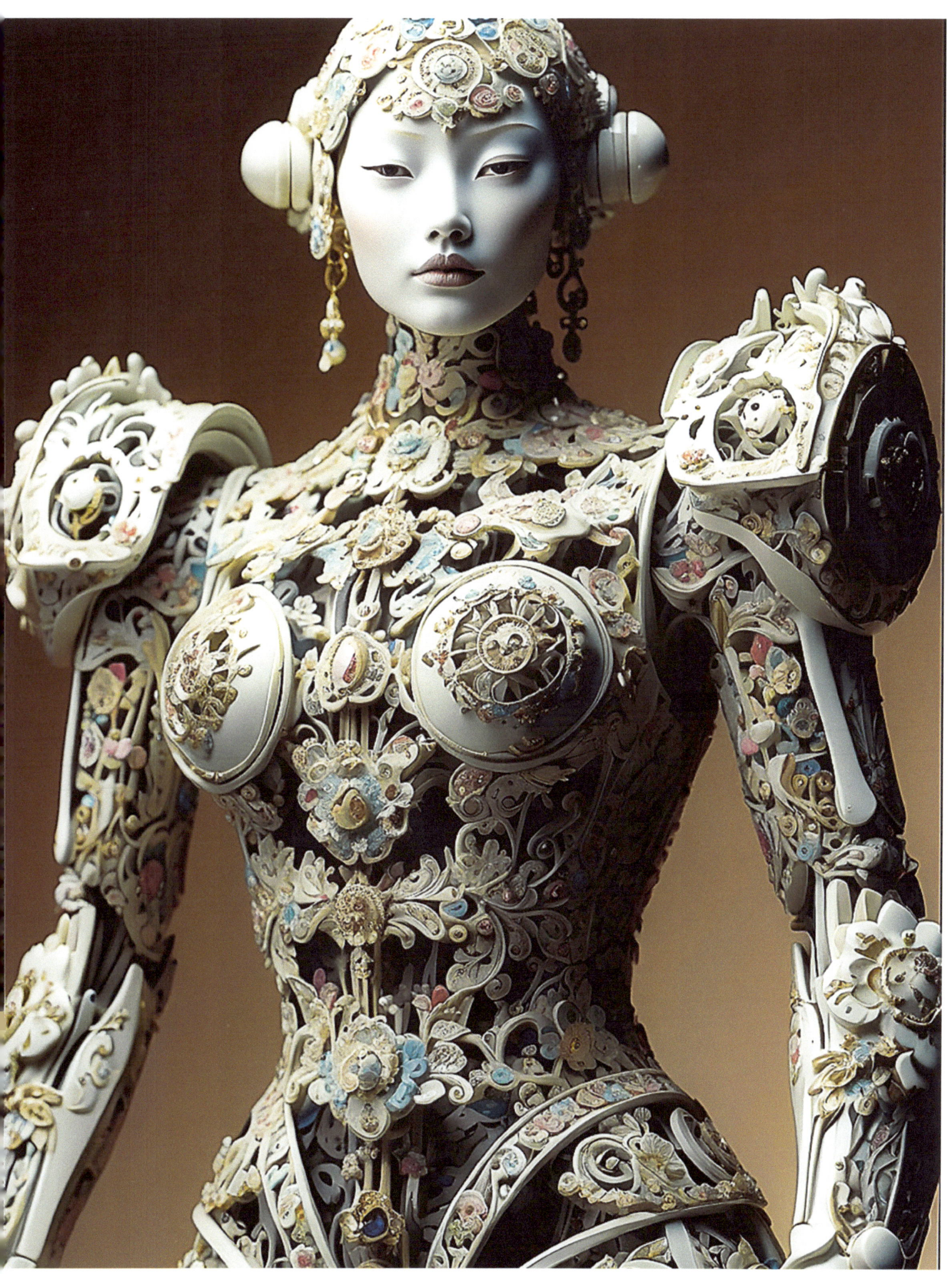

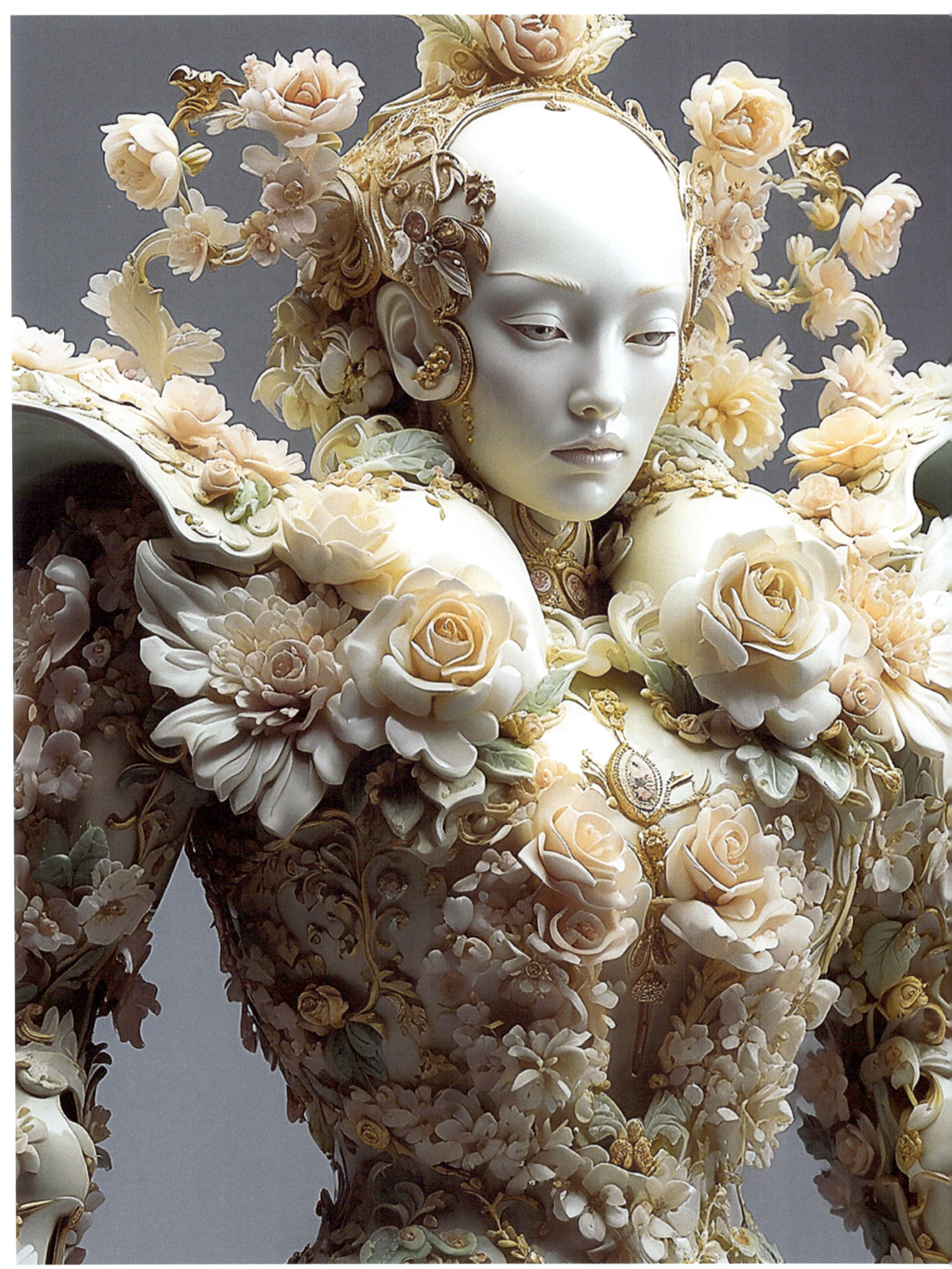

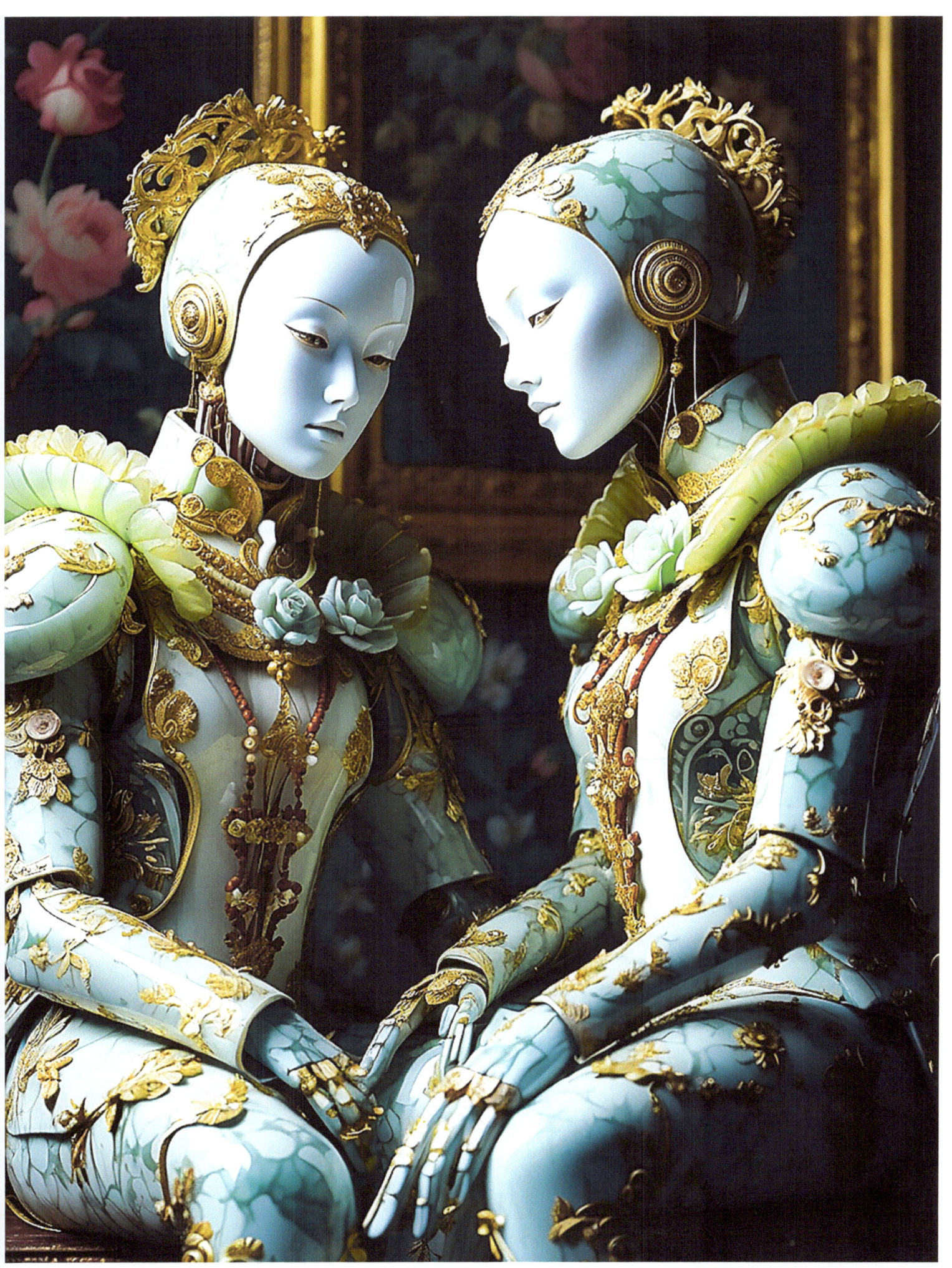

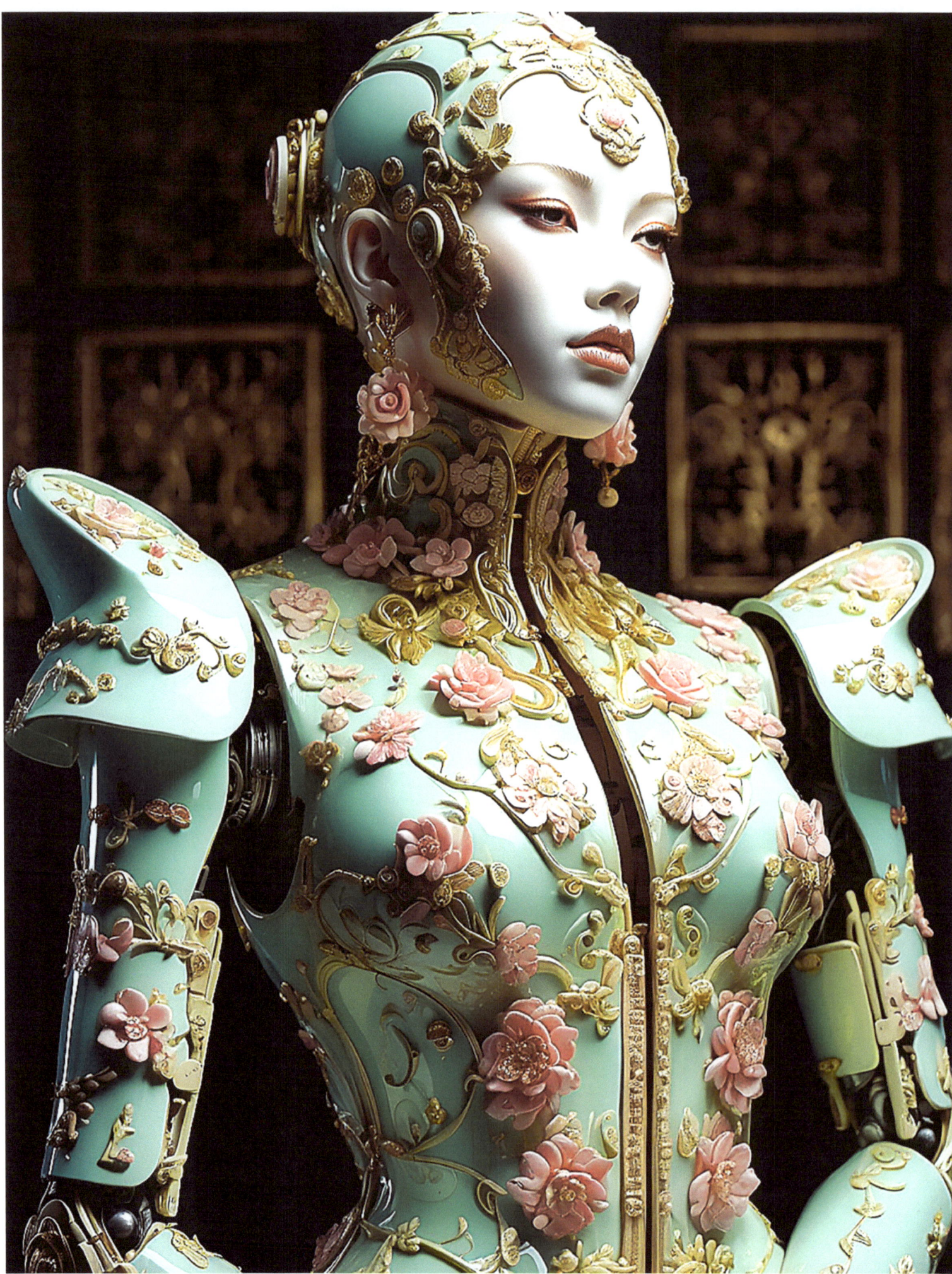

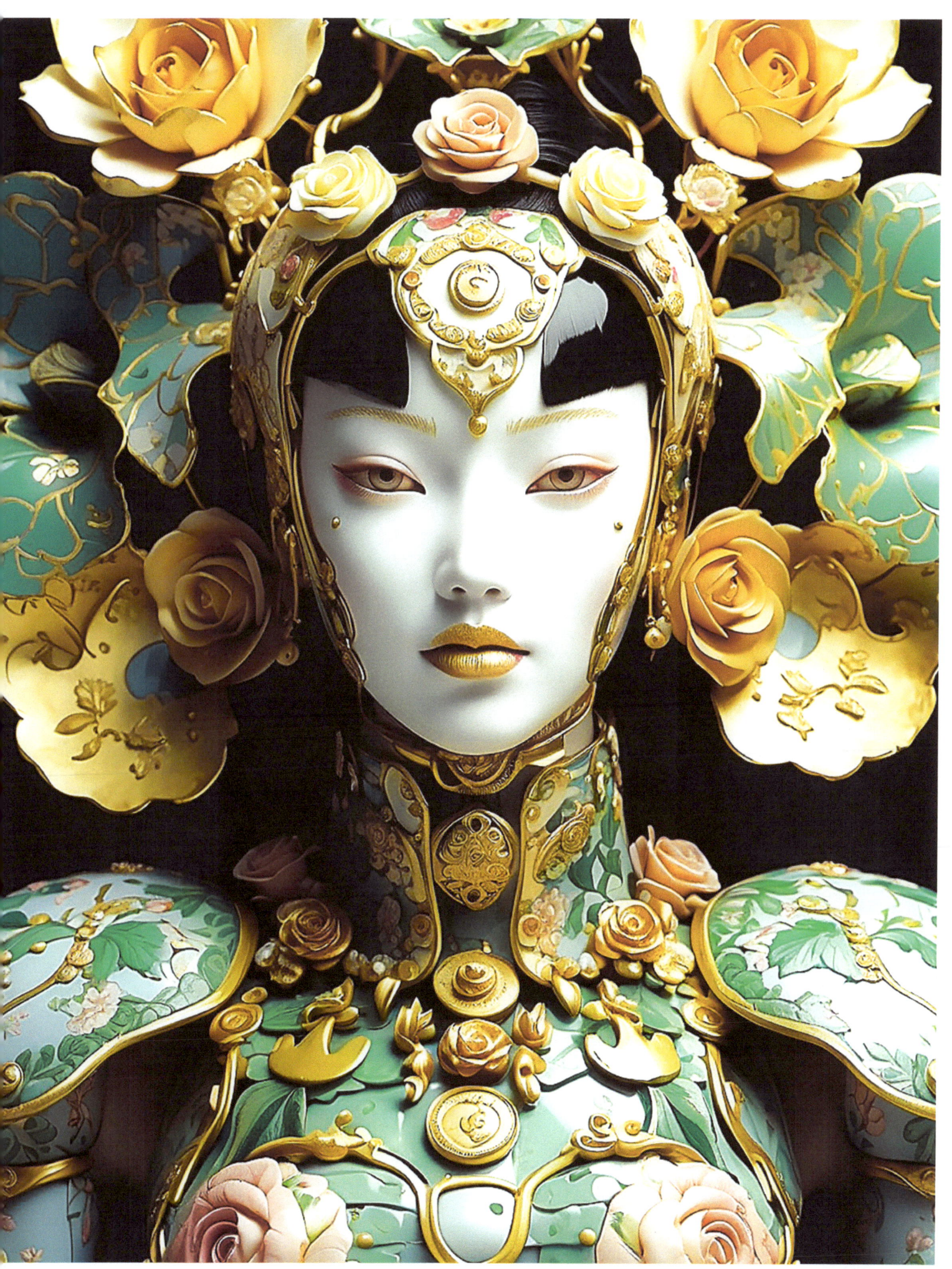

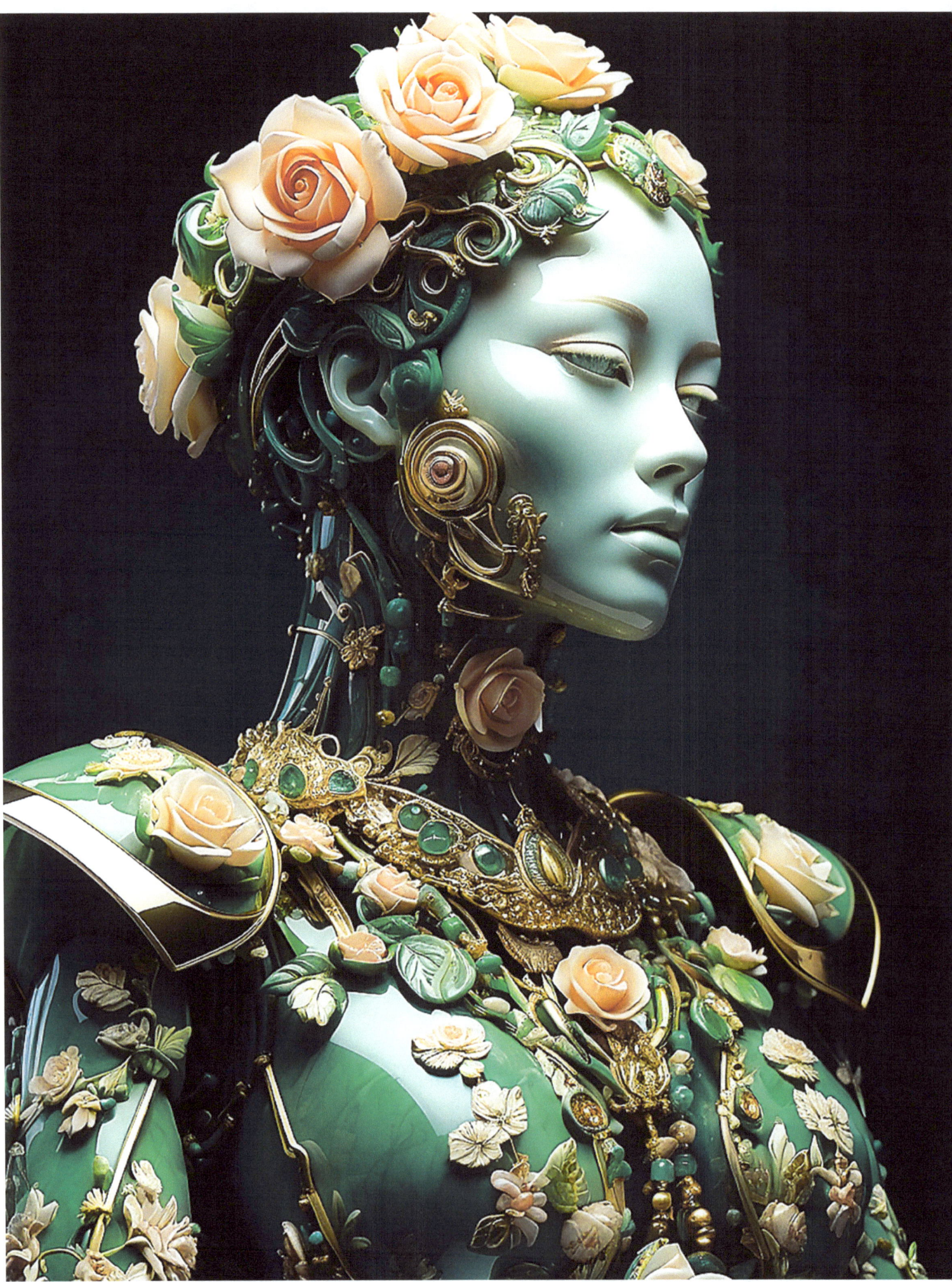

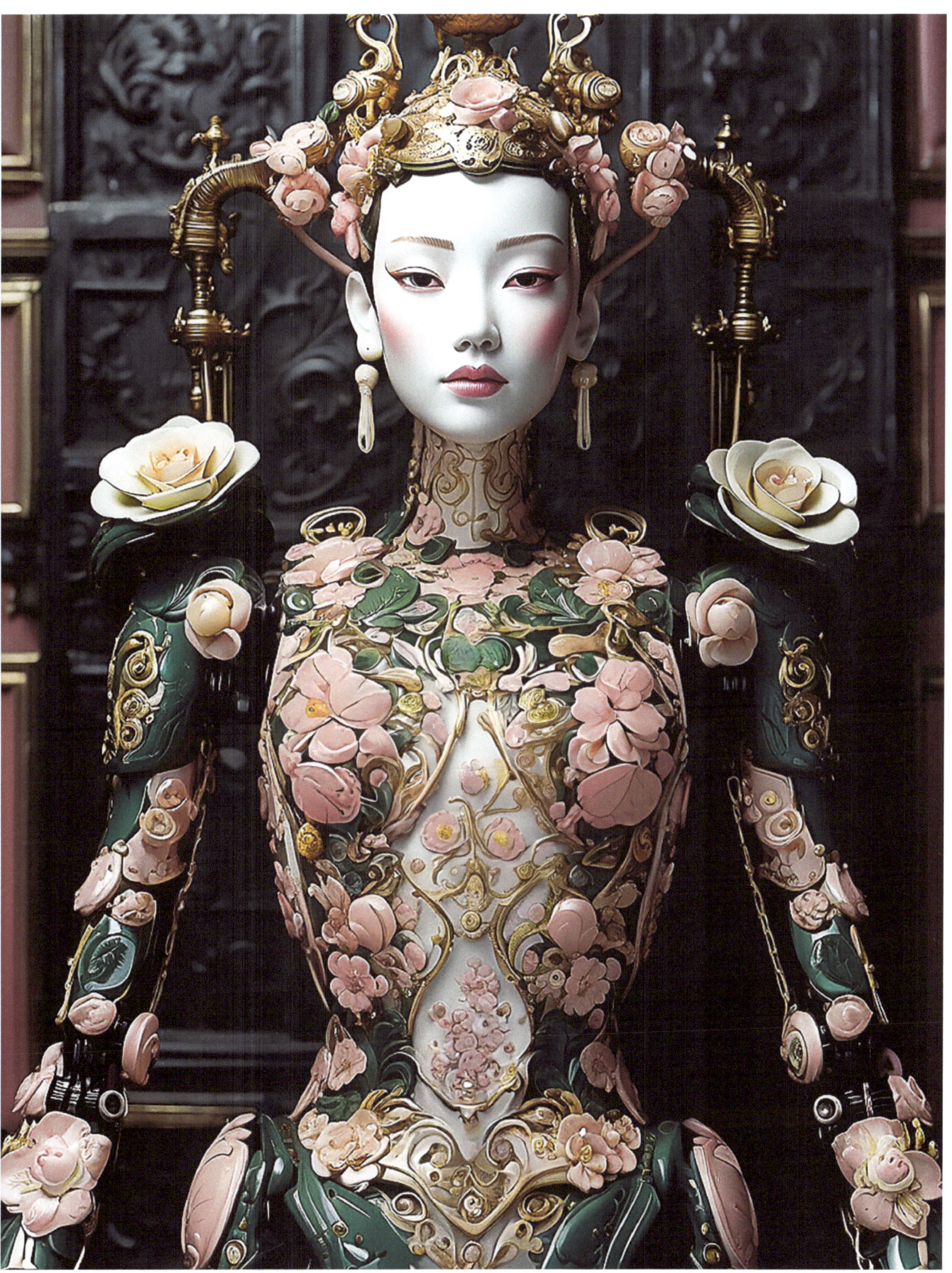

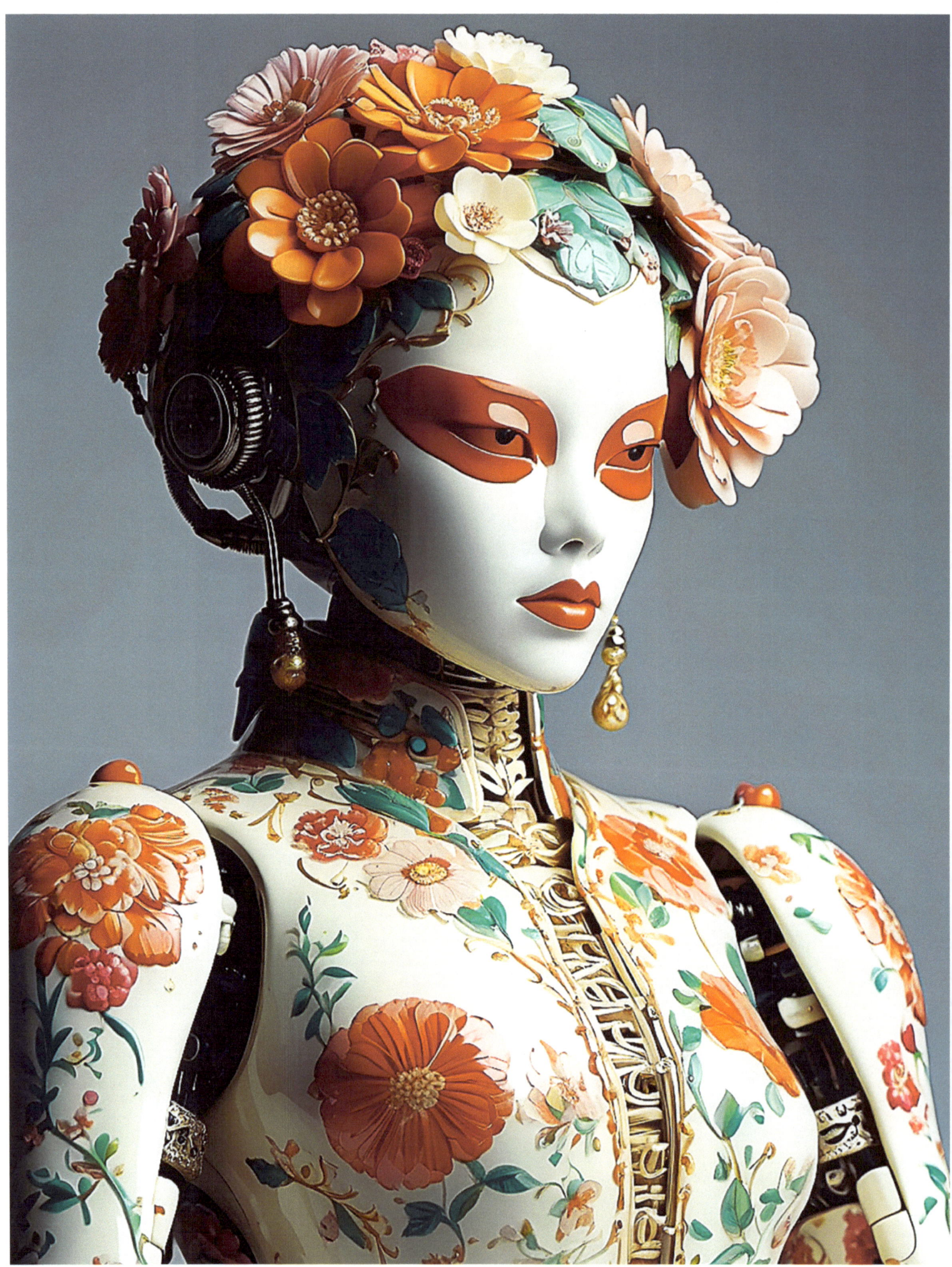

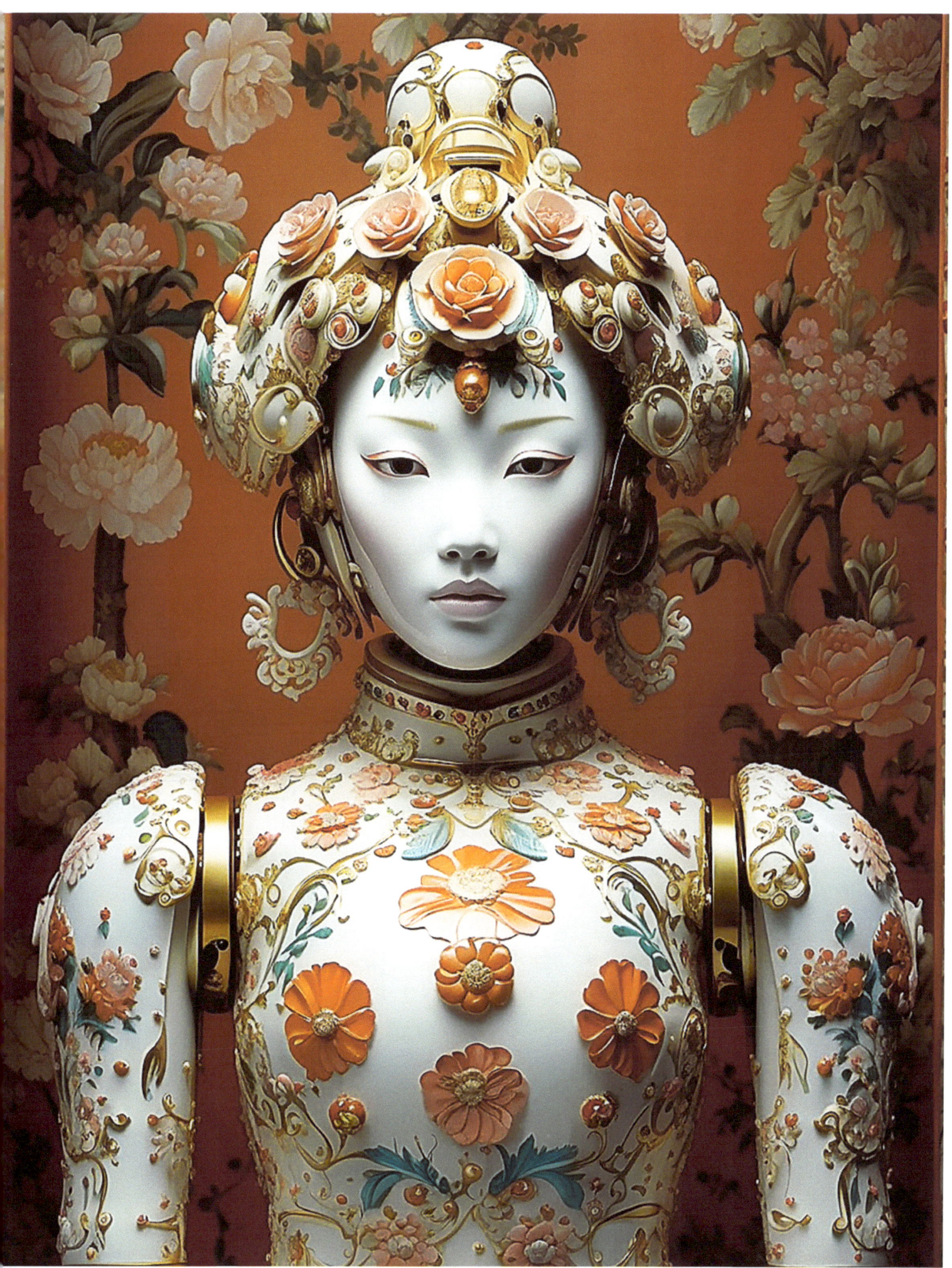

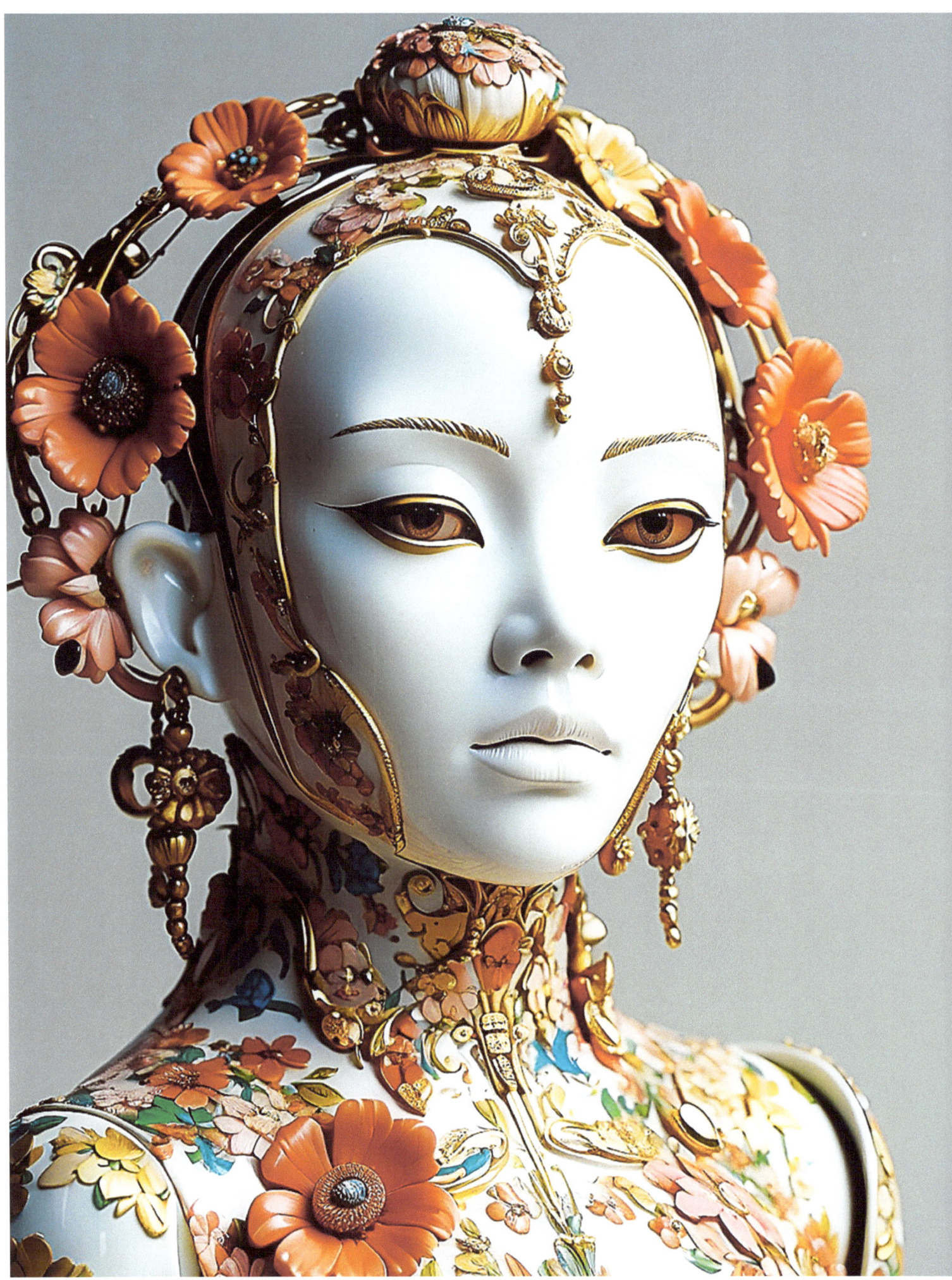

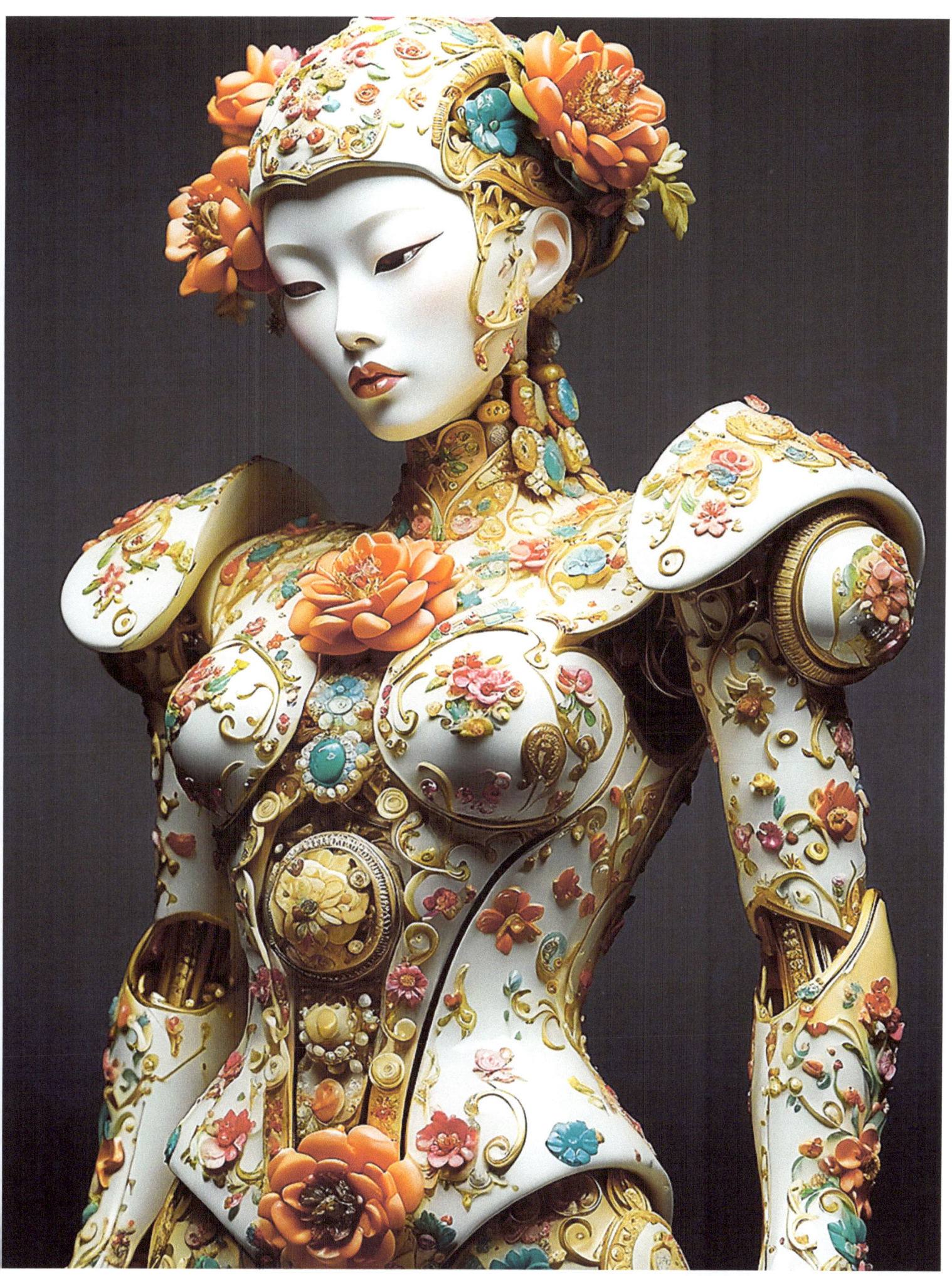

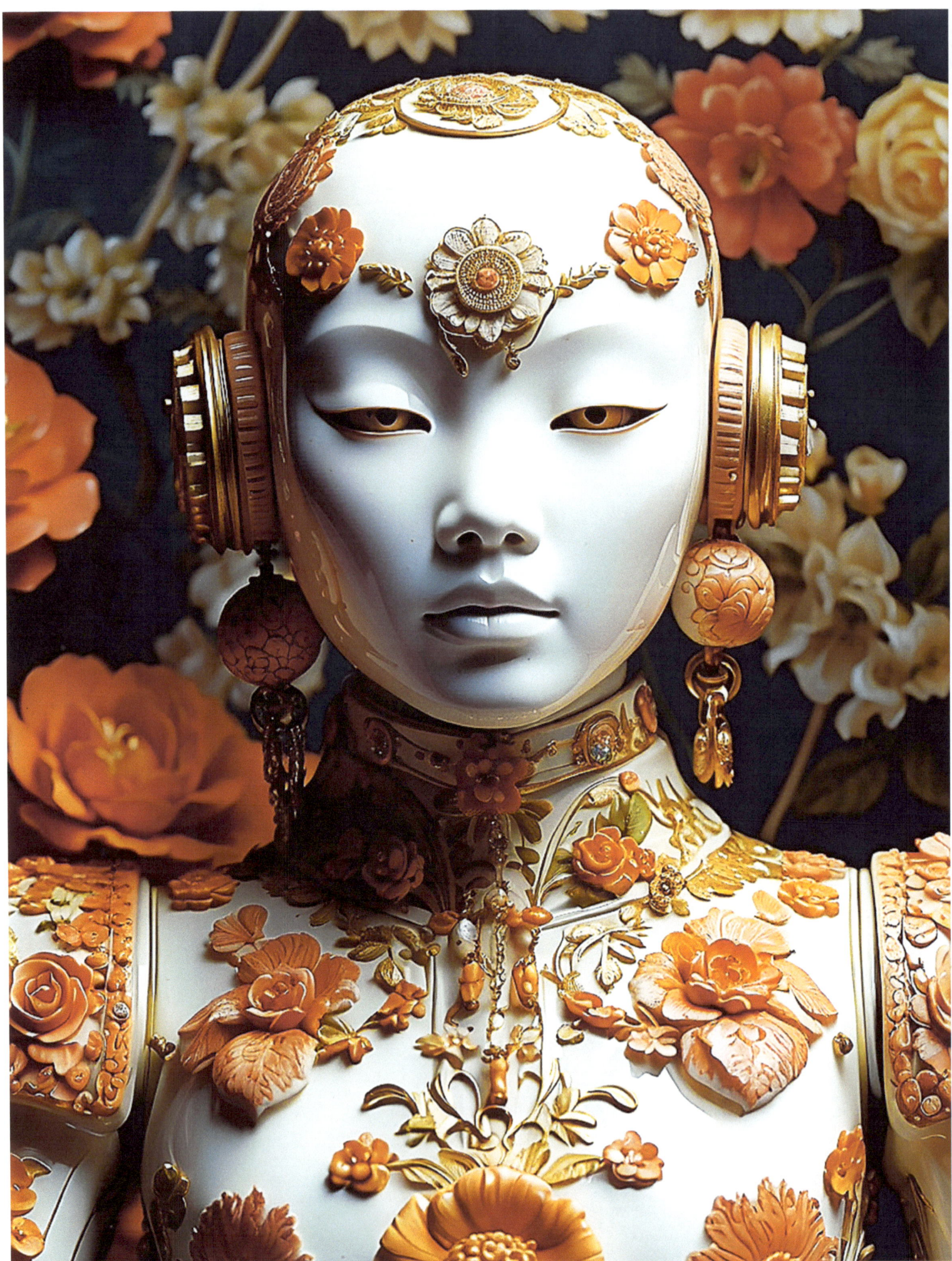

www.ingramcontent.com/pod-product-compliance
Lightning Source LLC
Chambersburg PA
CBHW051158220526
45473CB00003B/821